Continued Praise for *Man on a Mission*

"The life insurance industry has traditionally been male dominated. The landscape is changing as more women are entering the field and finding success using their unique strengths and skill sets. Learn from an industry icon on how to build confidence, systems and processes to create trusted relationships with prospects and clients."

—Jennifer Borislow, founder and president of Borislow Insurance and co-author of *Bend the Healthcare Trend*, past president of Million Dollar Round Table (MDRT)

"At a time when there are the fewest Life Insurance professionals in our lifetime, people own the least amount of personal life insurance in that same time frame while the need for Life Insurance professionals is greater than ever, Marv Feldman shares the secrets of the most successful Life Insurance family in the history of America! The unique insights that Marv shares took generations to develop and cannot be found anywhere else. Whether you are a brand new professional or have been in the business 30 years, you will get a fast track lesson to the top. Read this book, understand and apply the concepts and your success is assured. The impact you will have on the lives of your clients and their families will be even more rewarding!"

—Tom Hegna CLU, ChFC, CASL, Author and Speaker, President, TDH Financial Enterprises LLC

"Very worthwhile reading for anyone interested in building a successful career in this important industry."

—Michael Doughty, President & General Manager, John Hancock Insurance

"As an author of three books and high ranking recruiter in the life insurance based financial services industry, at this point there isn't a lot of commentary on the profession that gives me pause. This book does, and I believe it is the definitive work on the subject. By melding highly effective systems and practices with startlingly candid observations and experience, Marv Feldman lays bare an often-shrouded profession. His book makes it attractive, accessible, and is even compulsory to anyone considering a career that lets them have it all." It's the workbook we're all been waiting for!"

—Phillip C. Richards, CFP®, CLU, RHU,
Chairman of the Board of North Star Resource Group

About the Author
(continued from front flap)

A Million Dollar Round Table member for 42 years, serving as its president in 2002, Marv Feldman is also a 34-year member of MDRT's elite Top of the Table, serving on its board and as chairman.

Beginning his career in 1967 as an agent with New York Life in Columbus, Ohio, Marv transitioned to the company's management program, returning in 1974 to personal production in East Liverpool, Ohio, as a partner in the Feldman Agency and president of Fremar Financial Group.

Marv is very active in community activities having been a founder and director of the 1st National Community Bank and chairman of the East Liverpool City Hospital. He has co-chaired or chaired many advanced gifts campaigns for nonprofit, educational, and health organizations. Listed in Who's Who in Business and Finance and Who's Who in the World, he has spoken before industry audiences in 36 countries, been featured in key books and publications, and contributes to a variety of industry journals.

MAN ON
A MISSION

MAN ON
A MISSION

How to Succeed, Serve, and Make a Difference in Your Financial Services Career

Marvin H. Feldman, CLU, ChFC, RFC

978-0-692-68003-2 – hardcover
978-0-692-68004-9 – paperback
978-0-692-68005-6 – eBook

Library of Congress Control Number: 2016905191

For information, please contact:
Marv Feldman, mfeldman@lifehappens.org

Interior design by Dotti Albertine

CONTENTS

CHAPTER 1

Serve Well to Live Well

Success is about making a difference, not just about making money.

"Work hard. Think big. Listen well." That may sound like a Ben Franklin aphorism, but in fact it is attributed to my father, Ben Feldman.

Okay…so the Ben part is right. And undeniably, each had a black belt in achievement.

In order to understand who I am and where I came from, you need to appreciate what my father accomplished. This will help you understand exactly how I do what I do. If you are considering a career in the life insurance based financial services profession, the lessons I learned from my father which I will share with you can open unimaginable doors for your career. My goal in writing this book is not to teach you how to sell life insurance or financial services, but how to sell what they can do. Mastering this can create a life of service to others that serves you and your family as well.

But first, over the next 9 or 10 years we'll lose 40 percent of insurance agents and advisors to death, retirement, and normal attrition.

There are currently 300,000 licensed insurance professionals in the industry, so 120,000 will be leaving. Only 15 percent of new hires are retained at the end of four years, meaning we're going to lose 12,000 individuals a year.[1]

This means the industry needs to hire 80,000 agents a year just to stay even. Can you imagine what this means for a prospective agent or advisor? The opportunities will be tremendous.

As outstanding a job as my father did, when he entered the profession things were not as they are today. There was no welcome mat. Despite that, in his 51-year career, my father sold more than $81 billion in life insurance policies. One-third of these were after he turned 65. Industry experts and the media called him the greatest life insurance salesman of all time, and other sources credited him with being among the most prolific salespeople in world history.[2]

So how did he, the son of an immigrant poultry farmer and junk peddler from the hinterlands who seemed destined to follow his father as a farmer, transition to earning record-setting commissions, transforming an industry in the process?

What's more, along the way he managed to inspire two sons to share his passion for three things that are often missing on the sales front: ingenuity, integrity, and service. These elements are life-building tools as much for the agent or advisor as they are for the client.

If you're a Harry Potter fan, as is my family, you might be tempted to call what my father did wizardry, but upon closer examination, his kind of magic was practical, accessible, and transferrable. And while it may take time to master, it's an alchemy with three startlingly simple primary ingredients: earn an exceptional living, listen well, and serve others like no one else.

1 LIMRA *Agent Production and Retention Report,* 2008 and 2013.

2 "Ben Feldman, 81, Dies; Was Premier Salesman," *New York Times,* November 10, 1993, http://www.nytimes.com/1993/11/10/obituaries/ben-feldman-81-dies-was-premier-salesman.html.

* * * *

IF YOU BUILD IT...

Remember Roger Bannister? Until he set a record in 1954 by running a four-minute mile, for decades people presumed it couldn't be done. So nobody even tried. But within 46 days of Bannister's achieving this "unattainable" goal, others followed suit, and succeeded, doing what from practically time immemorial had been deemed impossible.

Our family's formula for achieving record insurance sales also defied convention and popular thinking and the seemingly impossible with its organic approach. If there was a sales barrier, we broke it, largely because **we never failed to get to know and understand our prospects to the core**. Who were they? How did they think? What qualities did they have? What made them tick?

We subordinated our own financial needs and goals to those of our clients, and at the end of the day, this netted us more revenue. We left dollars on the table, as I still do today, when it was in the client's best interest to do so based on product selection.

In short, what we do is **create money for the client where none existed before**. Taking days, weeks, or months to ascertain what the client is all about before that first meeting, and certainly during (ask questions about plaques on the walls, photographs, trophies, citations and awards, and the business they have created; become fluent in the client's vernacular) ensures that what you ultimately bring to the table will be compelling and emotional enough to work. Don't let anyone tell you anything different: in business or otherwise, decisions about money are fraught with emotion.

As agents and advisors, we are as much investigative journalists as we are or strive to be industry experts. **We are intelligence gatherers**. And based on the "evidence" we painstakingly root out, appealing to prospects on an emotional or "gut" level is what puts the proverbial magic in how the life insurance based financial services profession works.

. . . .

There are two basic emotions to which a client responds: fear and greed. Fear of personal, emotional, or financial loss. Greed because most prospects have worked a lifetime to earn their financial security. They don't want the tax man, confused family members, and poor planning by attorneys to destroy that security. Prospects respond to concept sales in these areas.

Today, too much industry training is based on product education (life insurance, mutual funds, annuities) rather than on **learning the psychology necessary to lay the groundwork and create an environment in which to sell these products.** In medical school, this would be equivalent to strictly learning how the body works as a machine to the exclusion of the *human* aspect of medicine—how to listen to the patient's wants and needs. This type of training is necessary for the doctor to become a skilled diagnostician. More and more medical schools are finally seeing the light about medicine and human communication, and implementing studies to that effect. So why is the insurance industry trailing behind? We also need to be crack diagnosticians. We need to listen not only to the prospects' wants and needs, but to their hopes, dreams, and desires to determine their areas of concern and deliver the appropriate solutions.

One of the resources you will find in this book is a list of questions to ask prospects which provide you with deeper insights into their real concerns and issues creating the right environment for you to solve the problems. **The products we sell are the solutions to these problems, but we must first disturb the prospect enough to make**

them aware that there are problems to solve. Then we can educate them as to how cost-efficient our products can be, especially in light of competing financial priorities. In this regard, and while we work toward attaining our own goals, we are providing a great service by enabling clients to take care of all that matters to them—their businesses, families, and communities.

Professionally, we all want to leave a legacy—best agent, best manager, leading producer—and we need the tools to accomplish these goals, which will be shared with you throughout this book. Along with experience in life and our industry comes a different perspective. As I matured and became a top producer, I wanted to be known not just as a leader in the industry but as someone who gives back to the industry and community, and as a loving husband, father, and, eventually, grandfather and to provide a balance between family values, productivity, and professionalism.

In today's Gen X and Millennial-defined world, expectations about giving back and work-life balance are shifting faster than ever. The idea of entering a profession that encourages you to serve others, make a difference in their lives and the lives of the people around them, and make a great living in the process, all while setting your schedule around your family life, is the blueprint for personal and professional success as I have come to know it.

* * * *

WHY DO PEOPLE BUY LIFE INSURANCE?

Would you buy a policy from someone who took up two hours of time you didn't have to spare showing you complicated information while knowing as much about you and your family as the cashier at the grocery store? Would you purchase something as significant as life insurance if the reasons put before you did not elicit a compelling reaction?

So why do people buy life insurance? Is it because of peer pressure? Of course not. Life insurance solves a problem they did not know they had until you uncovered and explained it to them. You took the time to learn about them first.

It may be a simple problem, such as paying off debt or paying for a funeral. Or perhaps it is paying for children to attend college and graduate school or have the wedding of their dreams. Perhaps it is fulfilling that long-held vision of starting a business, or ensuring the family will have sufficient income to maintain its lifestyle if one or both of the breadwinners are gone. It may be a more complex problem, such as business succession or estate planning, but in each event there is a problem that requires a solution.

In one particularly challenging case, I learned to never pass up the opportunity to sell term life insurance, something too many members of this industry downplay. This simple term sale lead to a multimillion-dollar permanent life insurance policy and a total of almost $100 million of life insurance on various family members.

* * * *

The CEO of a Fortune 500 company was introduced to my father by an insurance company's board of directors. Because this CEO had a strong foreign accent that my father found hard to understand, my father asked me to take over.

In time, I cultivated this individual into a client, writing coverage for him, his sons, and other family members. There was a significant amount of term life insurance written, but he would never address his own personal estate planning. In fact, he was so adamant about avoiding it, the many times I walked in with something on paper he'd proceed to throw it over his shoulder onto the floor. "Let's talk about something else," he'd insist. The message was clear.

About 10 years after he purchased the initial term insurance, I received an urgent phone call directing me to his home. He'd been diagnosed with a terminal illness and now wanted to finish his insurance planning.

Here, again, the magic of life insurance worked, as popular thought would lead one to believe that a terminal illness diagnosis was a rather formidable obstacle to writing a policy.

Because his wife was in perfect health, I contacted the chief underwriters of several companies to determine if survivorship life would work for this client. This was around the time second-to-die life insurance was coming into vogue. In a second-to-die policy, two people are insured under the same policy, but it doesn't pay a death benefit until the second insured dies. It was really designed for estate planning to absorb the tax on the second death.

Fortunately we were able to get them both insured using a survivorship whole life policy, with a $27 million death benefit. The policy was rated, but the premium was sustainable and affordable for the public corporation where my client worked. The client accepted the proposed policy, and we put the program into effect.

The original design was a collateral assignment split-dollar arrangement, with the trust as the owner and beneficiary, and the corporation receiving premiums paid. Several years after the policy was placed, Enron happened, along with subsequent changes in tax laws. As a result, we had to revise the original policy to an endorsement split-dollar arrangement, which meant the ownership of the policy changed from the trust to the corporation.

With this arrangement, you endorse the policy for the portion of the benefit that is going to be paid to the trust. In this case, the corporation would get a refund of all premiums paid, and the balance of the death benefit would be paid to the trust.

In essence, the net death benefit to the trust was exactly the same as before. An advantage for my client to using a survivorship split-dollar arrangement was that the economic benefit that he had to recognize was based on IRS Table 2 (Joint Life Expectancy). The Table 2 formula for $27 million of death benefit at his age amounted to less than $10,000 a year of taxable income. That was also what he had to report as a gift to the trust. This is quite different than if he were purchasing this policy directly with a $1 million premium. He would have to donate $1 million to the trust every year and then pay the gift tax on that, which would have amounted to another $500,000. So the split-dollar arrangement proved to be a very efficient way of providing the large sums of life insurance required to cover the payment of estate taxes.

As the gods would have it, my client went on to live almost 14 years after the policy was written. His wife passed away 18 months after he did. So here we had a policy that had $34 million worth of death benefit (having grown from the initial $27 million) that was now paid in 2010—at a time when there were no estate taxes. Due to a fleeting window where the government was trying to figure out what it wanted to do about taxes in that regard, the family received all the money earmarked for estate taxes to do with as they wished.

That said, in the months just before the wife died, there was a point where the company needed to renegotiate its lines of credit as the banks had limited their availability during this process. Many million dollars' worth of cash value in their corporate-owned policy was able to be accessed until they got their lines of credit renewed and were able to repay it.

In essence, we did multiple things with this policy: We provided the liquidity the family needed to pay estate taxes, though eventually they did not need to be paid due to tax law changes. And we provided cash for the corporation at a crucial time because it could not access its credit line. The magic of life insurance is we create money where none existed before using term and permanent insurance.

* * * *

BOOT CAMP AND BENEFITS

My response to probing questions about selling an intangible like life insurance is that I don't actually sell insurance. I sell money. **I sell dollars for pennies apiece.**

Toward the end of my father's career, his annual commissions exceeded $1 million a year, which at the time was the sum total of the entire sales forces' commissions at other companies. He did this in part by virtue of his ingenuity and creative persistence in getting himself in the door (face-to-face is always the goal), a feat which he taught me, where even many of the best salespeople often fail.

In my presentation kit is a page on which I glued a fanned-out stack of million dollar bills (no, they were not real) along with three pennies: dollars for pennies apiece. The million dollar bills represent the size of the client's problem. The pennies—the price tag for the solution. This page helped prospects visualize the size of their financial problem versus the cost of the solution.

My father's vision, insatiable thirst for evolving industry knowledge (guess how he spent his nights and weekends?), and acuity in creating liquidity where there was none were essential elements in his proficiency and success, and he passed it all on to me.

When I first entered the profession, I was straight out of college. I knew I was going into the business, but I wasn't sure what I was going to do and how I was going to do it. I grew up in the shadow of an extremely successful father who set the bar high with all kinds of global sales records, and my expectations were high.

Before I decided to join our industry, I wanted to see where else I might use my business, marketing, and economics degrees. I interviewed with IBM, Xerox, and General Motors, where they always seemed to ask the same two questions:

1. **How much money do you expect to make?**
2. **When do you expect to make it?**

Taking my cue from my father's (and many of his peers') stratospheric achievements, I'd give them an answer that generally elicited a belly-laugh response that, to paraphrase Ralph Waldo Emerson's famous Revolutionary War tagline about a shot fired, was something like "the laugh heard round the world." In that moment, I knew I wasn't destined for those industries. For all I know, those hiring managers are still laughing, but I'm not.

In what I consider insurance boot camp, and because no one sold mutual funds or other products we sell today, I spent two and a half years calling on newlyweds, brand-new parents, people buying new homes, and servicemen coming home that needed to convert their life insurance. I was surviving—newly married myself, making an honorable living, but just surviving. While I understood the technical aspects of life insurance from being around my father, I still had to learn how to sell the products.

One of the issues I had early in my career was proving to the industry and my family that I could succeed without my father's help. While working as an agent, if I had a good production month, everyone assumed my father had helped me by sharing cases. If I had a bad month, they gave me full credit.

Eventually, to prove I could be successful on my own and be in a position where my father could not be credited with helping me, I went into management with New York Life and started training other people. This allowed me to develop a different perspective on the sales process. In a sense, it was an early manifestation of my desire to serve people, as I could make sure the new agents benefitted from the wisdom I'd gained from many of my mistakes.

When my mother died in 1974, my father asked me to leave management with New York Life and come back to help him. He was in East Liverpool, Ohio, and I was 200 miles away in Columbus, Ohio. My brother Rich was already working with my father, but my father still wanted me to come back. So I did. My job when I was in Columbus was to train new people on how to make small sales to middle-market people. A $50,000 whole life sale, way back then, was a very large sale.

The first case my father asked me to work on was with somebody he had already had an appointment with.

"Marv, our personalities, this person's and mine, are not going to mesh," he'd said. "I think you'll do better. So here's the illustration; go back and present it."

He gave me an illustration for a million-dollar death benefit. I'd never presented a million-dollar death benefit. The only good thing I can say about that first interview is that I went. Nothing else happened.

But it was a great learning experience because it allowed me to expand my thinking—adding more zeroes onto the problem, more zeroes onto the solution, while knowing the solution is relevant and correct for a person in that position. It allowed me to understand the bigger numbers and not be afraid of presenting those bigger numbers. I once heard us described as "financial health specialists," which, if you'll excuse the expression, is right on the numbers.

That's one of the big areas for new people coming in: they're afraid to talk about the real numbers, the real solution, because it's so far out of line from their current thinking. **Realistically, it's a matter of acclimating, adjusting, understanding, knowing that if it's a $100,000 solution or a $10 million solution, you have the right solution for that person at that time,** and the cost is whatever the cost is. No one ever died with too much money.

* * * *

GIVE TO LIVE (WELL)

As I stated earlier, according to the 2015 *Insurance Barometer Study* by Life Happens and LIMRA, there are 234 million adults age 18 and older, with 100 million people having no life insurance.

Of those that do have some form of life insurance, only four out of ten own an individual life insurance policy.

Meanwhile, 30 percent of partnered/married households wish their spouse/partner would purchase more life insurance.[3]

And, according to a 2012 Genworth Lifejacket study, 40 percent of those who do have life insurance don't think they have enough.[4]

Over the next 9 or 10 years we'll lose 40 percent of insurance salespeople to death, retirement, and normal attrition. A Cerulli Associates study quoted in the November 23, 2015, issue of *InsuranceNewsNet* confirms that while the advisor headcount may have risen slightly in the past few years, the trend is short-lived, with a decline "at a more pronounced rate" set to start in 2020 "due to a major uptick in anticipated advisor retirements." It goes on to say that because the industry has acknowledged the loss of talent, "many industry stakeholders have introduced initiatives to engage recruits."[5]

According to LIMRA, only 30,000 to 34,000 agents are actually hired each year.[6] This is a problem…and an opportunity for you. The population base continues to grow. The middle class will move up the ladder. With fewer agents to serve them, you will have less competition and more prospects. But how do you reach them?

This book will show you how to benefit from this exceptional opportunity for growth and success and do good things at the same time. Young professionals want to know that they're making a difference in society, and you get to do that in this industry.

There are strategies that have worked for me over the years that

3 *Insurance Barometer Study,* Life Happens and LIMRA (2015).

4 *Getting Over the Gap: The 2012 LifeJacket Study,* Genworth (2012). https://www.genworth.com/dam/Americas/US/PDFs/Consumer/Product/LTC/140122D.pdf.

5 Linda Koco, "Advisor Headcount Ticks Up but a Decline Looms," *InsuranceNewsNet.* November 23, 2015, http://insurancenewsnet.com/innarticle/2015/11/23/advisor-headcount-ticks-upward-but-a-new-decline-is-looming.html.

6 Ashley Durham and Ben Baldwin. *Individual Life Insurance Sales Trends, 1975–2014—U.S.,* LIMRA Research (2015).

I will share with you. Among them are methods to expand your reach by harnessing the expertise of specialists in various fields, who can serve as experts on your team, and without whom you may not land a coveted client. I also present systems to implement in order to accomplish what you don't enjoy doing.

Do you love cold-calling? Neither do I, so I put someone in place who is equal to the task, focuses solely on the task, looks forward to the task, and makes a good living at it.

In business, playing to your strengths, and to the strengths of others, brings you to the finish line faster and far more efficiently than if you spent hours and hours forcing yourself to do something you dislike, or about which you are unsure.

. . . .

One day in the future, when you finally go out to pay a death benefit, sudden disability, or long-term care claim, in an instant you'll understand that everything you've done up to this time has taken you to this point, making a pivotal difference in someone's life. If earlier in your career you can accompany someone delivering a claim, you'll grasp the depth, scope, and gravity of this work that much sooner. You'll already be ahead of the game. But you have to know how to get there.

At one point in my career, I had the opportunity to write a disability policy for an individual who was originally a partner in a strong family business. After the patriarch passed away, unfortunately my client's brother ran the business into the ground. My client moved on to work for another company, but retained the life and disability insurance that had been purchased through the family business. In time, he developed coronary issues and was terminated from his job, unable to perform at the needed level.

In his early 60s, and suddenly without an income, he was able to draw on that disability policy, having a sufficient source of income until he passed away 18 months later. At that point, his life insurance came into play, giving his wife the capital she needed to maintain her standard of living.

This was an emotional time both for my client's spouse and for me. She was emotionally devastated by the illness and loss of her husband and the financial issues preceding his death. When she thanked me for all the years of service I had provided and on my insisting they retain the old policies, she was crying. So was I.

What this example illustrates is that when someone becomes disabled, or certainly when they pass away, other professionals can be like the proverbial wolf at the door, looking to get paid. **But because of your intelligence-gathering, diligence, and expertise, you're the one walking in with a check.**

In this industry, we solve problems for pennies on the dollar. We create money where none existed before, at a time when it's needed most. We create security, dignity, and peace of mind to keep the family and business together. Just like Harry Potter, the magic of life insurance is that it creates something where nothing existed before.

CHAPTER 2

Six Systems for Success

Prioritize and focus on first things first, because life rewards action.

There is no way to avoid doing hard work to achieve the level of success you want. If you enjoy doing certain tasks and are accomplished at them, clearly it will be easier to discipline yourself to perform them on a routine basis. **But for everything else, the keys to the kingdom are in creating and implementing systems that get the job done while freeing you to do what motivates you the most, and subsequently makes you the most effective.**

So many times in business we forget to look at the human side of work, which includes playing to our strengths for optimal results. If we don't like doing something, we will put it off. Discipline only goes so far. What are the chances of building a rewarding career performing endless tasks you don't look forward to tackling?

* * *

SYSTEM ONE: BREAKING THE ICE

Do you know someone who loves cold-calling so much every day that they leap out of bed and skip breakfast just to pick up the phone and dial? I may have met one or two of these people in my 50-year career, but I am not one of them. In fact, I was an extremely shy child who had to force myself to walk up to anyone and say hello. And when it came to my profession, I had, and continue to have, what is commonly known as severe "call reluctance." I'm human, and I don't like rejection. When it comes to picking up the phone, as Jack Nicholson famously said when rejecting an invitation from Shirley MacLaine in the film *Terms of Endearment*, "I'd rather stick needles in my eyes."

However, prospecting is imperative in maintaining and building this business, as it is for many businesses, so if you don't like it, find a way to do it without calling (and be sure to let me know what that method is). Or better yet, find someone who does it well and hire them.

In my quest for some kind of middle ground, my preferred way to prospect was not to pick up the phone right away but rather to research the prospect and send out a pre-approach letter, such as the ones that follow:

Dear _____ :

Most people aren't aware of the existence of the recent Gold Dollar Coin, like the one we've enclosed. Yet, it exists and has real value.

Similarly, most people aren't aware of our company, yet we do provide a service that other business owners and executives have found quite rewarding. Our services and our concepts are unique, and far more valuable than a One Dollar Coin.

I'd like to spend twenty minutes with you to show you what it is we do, and tell how it can be invaluable to you. I know that when you've seen our concepts and heard our ideas, you'll feel that your time was well spent.

We'll call you to arrange a mutually convenient time to get together. I'm looking forward to meeting with you.

Sincerely,

Marvin H. Feldman, CLU, ChFC, RFC

P.S. The above coin is very likely the only tax-free money you have received in some time. We would like to show you how you may get more.

Enclosure: Gold Dollar Coin

Sue Prospect
Wizard USA
28870 US 19N
Clearwater, FL 33761

Dear Ms. Prospect:

Financial and business planning is much like a chess match with the IRS. The chess pieces are your assets. You and your family win the match by strategic planning and keeping as many of the pieces as possible. The IRS tries to capture as many of the pieces as they can in the form of various taxes during your lifetime and upon your death.

Most people feel powerless against this monolith. Our services and our concepts are designed to help with your strategic planning in this game of chess.

I'd like to spend twenty minutes with you to show you what it is we do; and tell you how it can be invaluable to you.

I know that when you've seen our concepts and heard our ideas, you'll feel that your time was well spent.

We will call you to arrange a mutually convenient time to get together. I'm looking forward to meeting with you.

Sincerely,

Marvin H. Feldman, CLU, ChFC, RFC

Company Letterhead

Dear Referral,

Marvin Feldman of Feldman Financial Group recently completed a financial planning project for our company. Based on the quality of the work he performed, you may find his services of value.

While I don't know if these services will fit into your planning, I would suggest Marvin meet with you and Kathryn to discuss the financial programs which may be appropriate for you and your company.

Marvin will call in a few days to set up a convenient time to meet. I would appreciate your taking his call.

Sincerely,

Business Owner

Dear (Prospect):

The million-dollar bill gets your attention, doesn't it? That's because it's different than the money you see every day.

Our services and our concepts are different also, and far more valuable than a million-dollar bill.

I'd like to spend twenty minutes with you to show you what it is we do; and tell how it can be invaluable to you.

I know that when you've seen our concepts and heard our ideas, you'll feel that your time was well spent.

We will call you to arrange a mutually convenient time to get together. I'm looking forward to meeting with you.

Sincerely,

Marvin H. Feldman, CLU, ChFC

MF/b

Enclosure: Million Dollar Bill

In business, playing to your strengths, and to the strengths of others, brings you to the finish line faster and far more efficiently than if you spent hours and hours forcing yourself to do something you dislike or about which you are unsure.

Before Internet searches provided one-stop shopping for investigating a prospect, I used Dun & Bradstreet marketing reports. Today I use Google and Bing. These research sources would tell me if my prospect was a privately held company along with who owned the company and who the decision makers were. I would then send a personalized letter to whoever was at the helm.

Once I did that, a phone call was imminent. I've said I'm one of those people who, when the phone gets close to my ear, visualize a set of teeth about to clamp down on it, never to let go. However, after completing the first two or three calls, I could sit there all day making calls. It's like that first forkful of something you thought you didn't like, but once you try it again, you eat the whole plate. I admit to myself that I often never got to the point where I could pick up the fork, and neither do other agents who share my dislike for the process. If you don't make the calls, an egg timer can tell you how much longer you'll be in this business.

In my search for a system to handle all this, I learned of a firm that specialized in providing highly skilled personnel to make these kinds of calls. They developed the scripts; they did the training; they did all the things I didn't want to do. And they helped me hire the right individual from their skilled pool. Working off lists I'd purchased of privately held companies to which I'd already sent out the pre-approach letters, we developed a system where this individual would make appointments in specific geographical areas. Her compensation was based on appointments kept and clients acquired as a result of those meetings. (Caveat: it's best to work out a system where one specific geographical area is tackled at a time, so you don't spend your life in the car driving back and forth like a ping-pong ball.) This individual and I worked out the kinks and learned to work collaboratively, each of us with our own strengths, and productivity skyrocketed.

. . . .

SYSTEM TWO: THE PEN IS MIGHTIER...

Another essential system I effectively put into place in my business was **copious note-taking.** And if you think this is something obvious, mundane, or to which you can adhere loosely, like an on-again, off-again diet, you may want to think again.

A longtime agent and colleague of mine took on an extremely complex case some years back, so complex that he brought me in as an outside expert. After a couple of meetings with the client, we ascertained the problem, determined the solution, and decided upon the best course of action. Medicals were done and policies issued, and I flew back to help deliver the cases and reaffirm why we did what we did, and why it fit this particular client's needs.

A few years later, the client apparently ran into some financial difficulties. He contacted the insurance company claiming the information he'd received was fraudulent—that we had misrepresented what we had presented. He stated it had been presented to him as a "private pension plan," which tipped us off right away, as that is a term I *never* use. We believed he was getting information from someone else.

In any event, he wanted the policies rescinded and a refund of all the premiums paid, which were significant. He went so far as to file a formal complaint and threaten litigation against the other agent. I was not named, and in fact he didn't even recall who I was. The problem was the other agent had absolutely no notes in his files—no copies of anything that had transpired among the three of us. I, on the other hand, had taken copious notes and had copies of everything.

At my colleague's mildly panicked behest, I sent my notes and records to the appropriate decision makers in this matter, and they dismissed the claim. This was followed by the claimant going to the insurance carrier, which also examined my notes and dismissed everything. The claimant then went to the insurance commissioner for the state of Pennsylvania, who reviewed my notes and dismissed everything, saying the claimant did not have a legal issue he could pursue.

The point is, had I not taken comprehensive notes and kept records of everything we had done, including *why* we did it, there likely would have been a large claim that the other agent would have had to pay. In today's digital world, it is very easy to transcribe your notes using programs such as Dragon Speaks or a service such as Copy Talk. I can't stress how important it is for you to do this on a systematic and continuous basis.

* * * *

SYSTEM THREE: DON'T DROP THE BALL

Where systems are concerned, I cannot emphasize enough how imperative it is to **follow up with prospects**—especially if they've given a thumbs-up to your doing this the first time you contact them (always suggest you follow up in a designated amount of time). Of all the systems you may learn from this book, follow-up is one of the most significant in making your business as profitable as possible without starting up the cold-calling machinery all over again.

I call this a "tickler system." The easy part is putting a reminder in your calendar program today that pops up on your screen three months from now, six months from now, or a year from now, whatever you and the prospect decided on that will tell you on that scheduled date to make the follow-up call.

But that's just the technology part.

The human part is not putting off the call, which at that point is more of a "warm" call than a cold call, because you have already connected with the prospect. Maybe the first time it was just bad timing, the solution presented wasn't right, the issue you'd thought was the problem wasn't the real problem, or it wasn't as severe as you'd thought it was. There are so many objections people can have. But as long as I'd left that first meeting on good terms, I felt fine about calling back.

There have been times when it wasn't a good first encounter, even if the prospect had left the door open for me to try again in the future. Under those circumstances, I'd have my assistant call. (Yes, I have call reluctance.) But in any case, I followed up.

There was one case where I had taken a considerable amount of time at an initial meeting to go into great detail about what I considered an appropriate solution for a prospect. Because I failed to follow up in the time frame promised, by the time I did call him back he thanked me for all of the information I'd provided and informed me that in the interim another agent had contacted him. Being well informed already, thanks to my first effort, he told me he gave the business to the other agent.

That was a mistake from which I learned a powerful lesson. No one has a 100 percent closing ratio—no matter what they tell you. In fact, mine was one out of three, but it could have been higher had I followed up with that prospect when I said I would. People look at me and see the success I've had over a long career. They see the leadership positions I've held and say, "Oh, Marv never has these kinds of issues. He never has these problems. He can't relate to what I go through." But that's absolutely false. I've had all the same issues, all the same problems, all the same challenges, all the same lessons to learn, all the same objections other agents and advisors hear every day.

Sometimes I was successful in overcoming objections and sometimes I wasn't. You don't get every case you work on. **But if you are disciplined and diligent in following up, even if it takes years, you will be successful in closing many more cases.** I can tell you for certain you'll get a lot more. It's the rare prospect that doesn't recognize persistence and promptness, because chances are that's how they've gotten to where they are as well.

∎ ∎ ∎ ∎

SYSTEM FOUR: THE ABCs OF EFFICIENCY

The maxim that "80 percent of your income comes from 20 percent of your clients" holds true, probably in most industries, and definitely in ours. Systems-wise, **you need to prioritize by picking and choosing the clients with whom you are going to spend the most time—your A, B, and C level clients. Otherwise, you can end up with a client who doesn't generate much revenue for your company but who takes up a huge chunk of your day, week, and month.**

As professionals we have to learn when it is more productive to say, "We are happy to help you, and you will be working with Barb on my staff," or "For what you want, the best option is to visit this web site, or call this 800 number as they can provide you with the kind of information you need more directly and comprehensively than we can." **You need to train your clients in how *you* work,** and how effective that makes your firm in being able to satisfy everyone's needs in a timely manner, including theirs. **So much of being effective in the life insurance based financial services profession is about**

mastering the art of "it's not so much what you say, it's how you say it." This clearly applies to training clients to perceive information in a positive light.

Where staff is concerned, efficiency matters too. At its peak my office had 55 people. We had a lot of outside activities, such as real estate, gas and oil partnerships, and property management that weren't related to the field of insurance and investments. I can recall the day when I went to my father and brother, explaining that because of this outside activity we'd taken on, I was losing my client focus. I suspected we all were.

I had personally taken on a great deal of these interests and other preoccupations that had found their way to us due to revenue we needed to invest. You put your mind where your money is. I firmly believed our clients were getting shortchanged. We decided to sell or close anything that didn't enhance our core business of insurance and investments, cutting our staff from 55 to 13.

Similarly, in a sweeping effort to return Apple to profitability in 1998, Steve Jobs made a decision to hone its glut of products down from 350 to 10 so the company could focus on excellence. They soon began developing again, which improved the bottom line.[7] As for us, while our gross was considerably less than Apple's, our bottom line did go way up.

So a system that enables you to key in, focus, and run your business in the most efficient, productive, powerful way possible is one more step forward on the road to achievement in this industry.

* * * *

7 Carmine Gallo, "Steve Jobs: Get Rid of the Crappy Stuff," *Forbes*. May 16, 2011, http://www.forbes.com/sites/carminegallo/2011/05/16/steve-jobs-get-rid-of-the-crappy-stuff/.

SYSTEM FIVE: HARNESSING THE TEAM

There are nearly 1,000 companies in the life insurance industry, and each company has its own products. They may be a version of a whole life product, a universal life product, an index life product, or annuities, and so on. We can't possibly know everything about all of these products. You just can't be all things to all people. In fact, if that's what you decide to try, you'll spread yourself so thin you'll be of no use to anyone.

The magic of harnessing a team of specialists to help grow your business is taking the time to know who knows what—and how well they know it. Identify your experts, the CPAs, attorneys, bankers, pension experts, and insurance company wholesalers and product specialists, whether they work for you or are outside of your business. Cultivate relationships with the understanding that you can help each other in the acquisition of clients.

Too many times, especially when agents are starting out, there is a tendency not to want to give up any part of a commission. But given the complexity and diversity of the life insurance and financial services industry, and its overabundance of specialties and products, it may cost you the client.

In an effort to be all things to all clients, I've seen many agents and advisors go in saying, "I've searched the market and here are the 17 companies and products that fit your requirements." You can see the client's eyes glaze over because no one wants to look at a massive spreadsheet with all those elements. What the client expects you to do is expertly research the market and come back with two or three options at most, and your recommendation of the single solution you believe is best.

In the quest to make that recommendation, it is wise to harness the expertise of individuals who may have a better handle on these companies or products, whether they participate with you in the meeting or stay behind the scenes. **You don't have to be an expert in everything, but you do need to know where to find the answers.**

. . . .

SYSTEM SIX: A FAMILY AFFAIR

In case you're wondering where your family fits in as you work to make your business thrive, the answer is: everywhere.

One of the things which I'm keenly aware of in this business is that it can absorb all of your time and energy to the detriment of your family. In fact, I learned early on that attending a meeting or seminar and asking a colleague how a spouse was—using that spouse's name—could cause some embarrassment. All too often, a separation or divorce had occurred, maybe because of the business, and perhaps the colleague was on husband or wife number two or three. Asking "How's the family?" put me on safer ground. (On one occasion, the agent actually thanked me for my choice of words!)

In Chapter 8 I delve into the family's role in this industry in more detail, but fundamentally, establishing a schedule that includes family time and family values will serve you in the best possible ways.

My mother had a rule that on Friday nights everyone had to be home for dinner, most emphatically my father. Likewise, when my wife and I decided to get married, we also recognized that I may need to invest 12, 14, 16, or even 18 hours a day in my work, but Friday nights were for family dinners, and weekends were for my wife and me on one day and the children on the other. Of course there were exceptions, for instance, when a client passed away and a funeral was held on a weekend. But overall, your family needs to be a central part of your team. In this way, expectations are met and the time and energy you have to invest in business is not impacted by unhappiness, disappointment, and resentment at home—which can translate to ineffectiveness with clients.

. . . .

Achieving success in this industry is a choice and a plan, and how you run your business in pursuit of success is also a choice and a plan. While nothing is foolproof, breaking that plan down into reliable systems provides a strong foundation, freeing you up to do what you do best. It gives you the opportunity to work hard, work smart, think big, and listen well.

CHAPTER 3

You Must Invest Money—and More— In Your Business to Make Money

You must first sell yourself. Buy more products yourself.
Then propose more and you will close more.

Investire—**Latin for** "to clothe in, cover, surround."

In the life insurance industry, which involves a great breadth and scope of investing, **the one you make in yourself and your business is the cornerstone for everything else that follows.**

Fundamentally, investing in whatever it takes to build your business should be a series of priorities that evolve and grow as your business does. These investments may not be strictly monetary in nature: the kinds of investments I'm talking about run the gamut from technology to staff to education and products to more altruistic pursuits where an investment in the greater good of your community can serve it (and sometimes you) in unanticipated ways.

Let's start with technology.

Aside from investing in the office and industry-related software that will facilitate a manageable work flow for day-to-day tasks, investing in staff that is competent in or can be trained to use that technology will free you up to do what you need to do on a larger scale. In the realm of social media, if you are not comfortable with it, you'll want to make sure you've hired support staff that can regularly feed and maneuver your social media accounts to enhance your cyber presence, allowing you to spend more time on the phone and in front of clients. The brochure at the end of this chapter addresses common mistakes agents and advisors make, among them (mistake #1 and mistake #5) the failure to effectively strategize the use of e-mail, texting, video conferencing, and social media.

One of the most efficient ways to initiate a social media presence is to use resources such as those provided by Life Happens **(www. lifehappens.org)**. You and your staff can access a team of social media experts and video resources to provide you the tools needed to help your prospects and clients make insurance-related planning decisions. Using social media isn't about reinventing the wheel. It's about finding the right tools to make sure your presence is noticed.

While delegating to the right team members is important, it doesn't mean letting go completely. Do your homework to find out what programs, tools, and methods other companies use to their advantage, and bring them to yours. Ask around, read professional and business journals, and attend seminars and workshops (or delegate and send a qualified support staff person) to learn about new resources that can make your business shine in the realms of efficiency and overall marketplace presence.

If you are sitting at your desk pushing papers and filling out forms, these activities are preventing you from interacting with prospects and clients, or working on a host of other pursuits to grow your business. You know where your strengths and energies are best directed. Anything else is an obstacle that prevents you from being out there, face-to-face with the people you need to see and service. If something can be delegated to staff and/or assigned to technology without losing a personal connection to prospects and clients, it should be.

I have found over the years that the most effective means of delegating involves an investment of time when a task is initially assigned. Then, later, if a staff member isn't performing the way you want, rather than chastising them, maintain a positive approach that gives them the time and space to comprehend why you want something done a particular way. It doesn't matter if you have 2 or 52 employees, **when individuals are made to feel like part of the team, rather than just taking orders, they're going to want to make sure you succeed.** That will be *their* investment, and it will be made willingly.

* * * *

YOU MUST INVEST MONEY—AND MORE— IN YOUR BUSINESS TO MAKE MONEY

Some years ago, my brother and I decided to open a remote financial planning office in Youngstown, Ohio, about 50 miles from my primary office in East Liverpool. It was a good two hours round trip for me to commute every day while trying to run two offices in the process, so I hired an attorney, a paralegal, and a CPA to staff the remote office to work with our financial planning clients. We owned the building complex, and we invested a lot of time and money in designing and equipping the office itself. About a week before we were scheduled to open, the attorney I'd hired told me he'd be uncomfortable selling or marketing anything. Of course, in the financial services industry, most everything revolves around sales and/or fee planning.

I was left with a paralegal, who ended up being a superb staff member, and a CPA, who proved to be ineffective. I soon hired another

CPA who was quite sales-oriented, until that relationship ended, as they can over time.

At that point, my wife, Vicki, who was my corporate pilot for a number of years, decided we should invest in her to obtain a Series 7 license so she could take over the financial planning responsibilities in the Youngstown office.

What makes this part of the story even more compelling is that, even though I'd made every effort to help my wife and daughters understand how and why I make the time-consuming business decisions I sometimes do, or endure a less-than-cordial client, my wife's involvement in the business changed her view of why I did what I did. The investment in her continuing education and required licenses made her an integral part of the team, resulting in an even deeper level of understanding.

Working closely with clients, perceiving why they said or did certain things, or took certain actions, negative or otherwise, gave my wife a whole new perspective on the business. The investment in Vicki's securities licenses was a good one, and while not all spouses have an interest in joining the life insurance and financial services industry, she did and became a real asset: a valuable member of the team.

* * * *

One of the things new agents and advisors need to understand is that, if they're going to call on someone who has been successful, and they are dressed in inexpensive clothing that's showing its age, or driving a clunker of a car, they may lose the sale—in the first minute or less. According to *Forbes*, it may actually take as little as seven seconds.[8]

---

8 Carol Kinsey Gorman, "Seven Seconds to Make a First Impression," *Forbes.* February 13, 2011, http://www.forbes.com/sites/carolkinseygoman/2011/02/13/seven-seconds-to-make-a-first-impression/.

Unfortunately, we live in a society that judges books by their covers, especially in business, so an investment in how you present yourself is one of the keys to starting a solid relationship.

Aesthetics aside, it's important for new agents and advisors to understand that **if they are going to sell something, they need to first own it themselves.** If you're going to sell long-term care or disability insurance, you'd better own it. The same applies to whole life policies, universal life, and other products and services. Everything I presented to my clients as possible solutions I owned myself. I bought life insurance for my wife; I bought permanent life insurance for my children; I bought whole life policies for all of my grandchildren. I'm still paying the premiums on them as a gift to my family, but the bottom line is you have to believe in what you're selling.

If you don't believe in what you are selling enough to own it, and you're going to present it to a client who asks if you have it yourself, needless to say the writing's on the wall about how that meeting will likely end.

My father invested in whole life insurance policies for me when I was very young. A few years after my wife and I got married, we decided to buy a house. I'd only been working a couple of years, fresh out of college, so while my income wasn't great there was a source of money. That source was the cash values of my whole life policies, which I had taken over in terms of paying the premiums, and from which I borrowed to obtain the down payment on our first home.

When my children were born, my wife and I bought whole life policies for them, as did my father. When it came time for college and law school, part of the source of funding for their education came from the cash values of those policies.

As I move closer to retirement, I may use those cash values as an income supplement. It all goes full circle, **and the investment in these**

policies that you make when starting your life insurance business cannot be underestimated.

. . . .

In Chapter 2, I talked about implementing systems to make your business run like a well-oiled machine. Among those systems is harnessing the expertise of those whose skills may be outside the realm of your specialty. When I bring in an outside expert, it's an investment in that I'm sharing part of the potential revenue so I can more effectively deal with the concerns and issues of the client or even acquire the client in the first place.

Many times an agent or advisor says, "I don't want to give anything up. I'm going to do it all myself." But by doing it themselves, they don't always provide appropriate solutions for the client. They are not as effective as they could be. Additionally, the agent or advisor leaves themselves exposed if another agent walks in the door behind them and the client finds out you didn't fully inform them—the repercussions may be more serious than just sacrificing a portion of the fee or commission.

Over the years, whether I engaged an outside expert or not, I've sometimes left a tremendous amount of potential income on the table. I did this when I knew it wasn't right to recommend a program just because it would generate the most revenue for me. It was a sacrifice, which in itself is a form of investment. And it's an **ethical investment** as well, because if the client believes I've treated them fairly and learns to trust my judgment, the door will be open to future transactions between us and other potential clients they may recommend.

. . . .

One of the things I cannot stress enough in the realm of investing in your business is **continuing education**. As your children grow up, education gives them wings, and it can do the same for you. Just because we may have graduated from college or received an advanced degree before going into this business doesn't mean we should stop learning.

While I expand on continuing education and obtaining designations in Chapter 10, **an ongoing investment in knowledge can mean the difference between a business that sustains and one that soars.** If your office technology is state of the art, shouldn't your level of knowledge be the same?

Along the way, I've known a number of new agents and advisors who shun going to educational seminars and conferences, reasoning that their finances don't support it. While it's true that you may have to cover hotel, airfare, rental car, gas, meals, registration, and more, being on the cutting edge of this industry takes a strategic investment of this kind.

Today, you can do a lot of this on the Internet. There are webinars, podcasts, TED Talks, and so much more. But there is no price to be put on the advantage of face-to-face interactions with other people in the profession, which is only made possible by attending seminars and conferences. I can't even count the number of times I went to a conference that served me well, but the fact is I learned just as much or more interacting with other attendees by asking questions, sharing information, and brainstorming. On more than one occasion I also made invaluable contacts: experts in their respective fields whom I could call for help with a client when I determined my expertise wasn't enough.

Going to a meeting where CPAs and attorneys are providing estate or pension planning information can add to your repository, giving you that edge when meeting with a client. It never hurts to be able to reference a conference you just attended at the Heckerling Institute on Estate Planning in Coral Gables, or what you learned at a Million Dollar Round Table meeting in Vancouver, Canada. **What this tells the client is that you're motivated enough to invest the time, energy, and money to make yourself as qualified a professional as possible—one who is equal to the task of solving the client's problems and addressing all of their issues.**

● ● ● ●

We all want to make it to the top. We all want to be considered winners. If we're new to the industry, proving ourselves to clients and managers by building a successful track record is how we thrive and further our careers. In academia it's called "publish or perish." In Las Vegas, if you're in hotel sales, it's known as "landing the casino whale." One of the problems I've seen for someone coming into the life insurance business is that they very quickly write what I call a "jumbo" or "elephant-sized" case, one with a lot of zeros on both the problem and the solution. While that kind of achievement is certainly impressive, it is sometimes accompanied by the belief that all their cases should be comparable in size.

For the record, those really big cases are few and far between. They take a tremendous amount of time to develop from beginning to end. So if a new agent or advisor decides to concentrate strictly on pursuing them, it's just a matter of time before they'll be out of the business because they are not generating important day-to-day revenue. Investing time and energy in building your practice is just as important as investing time and energy in landing the whale. It's true that that kind of client will gain you notoriety, maybe enable you to purchase the new car you need to present a better image, put a down payment on a house, or take a family vacation. But what's going to pay the bills and buy the time you need to acquire the dream is your investment in writing the day-to-day cases.

· · · ·

Growing up, being part of a group or team like Boy Scouts or Pop Warner is something to look forward to. What child doesn't relish being in a circle of like-minded friends and acquaintances with so much to achieve, maybe even serving others in the process? We allocated a great deal of time and energy and probably had a lot of fun along the way and may not have understood these pursuits as the investments they were.

As adults, while our concept of fun may have changed, joining various organizations is an investment that can pay dividends in terms of bettering our communities, our families, our businesses, and ourselves. That said, joining an organization solely for the purpose of finding out "what's in it for me" is a bad investment. I have found that when my objective is service and my intentions decidedly altruistic, the rest usually takes care of itself.

When I still lived in Ohio, I was asked to join a hospital board of directors. I thought long and hard about it because I was already committed to other organizations, but the hospital was trying in earnest to improve itself. I told them I would do it as long as the time commitment was minimal, reasoning that it was an investment I could make in my community. The next thing I knew, I was serving on additional hospital committees and soon became chairman of the board. But all for a good cause!

The point is, when I invested my time in these community responsibilities, I had no intention of using them as a springboard for my business. My goal was purely to help people and organizations better themselves. But by virtue of this involvement, my efficacy and business acumen were under a microscope, and over time other professionals who were involved sought my counsel for their insurance and investment matters.

Of course, when you become involved in a nonprofit organization, you can expect to write checks to the same (how can you say no?). But, taking my own best investment advice, I purchased a life insurance policy making the hospital owner and beneficiary. Someday, when I am gone, the hospital is going to get a sum of life insurance that will go to the general hospital fund or another fund of their designation. This example illustrates the benefits of investing in life insurance not just for personal use, but as a tool for philanthropy. In fact, I have three separate organizations for which I've purchased permanent life insurance, and I've shared this with clients many times when trying to find solutions to their problems. Remember, if you don't own it, you probably can't sell it.

When working with high-net-worth individuals, I often ask if they want to leave a legacy, without spending all their money to do so today. I can show them a way to do this for pennies on the dollar. Buy a life insurance policy for a nominal premium, owned by and paid by that charitable organization through the client's personal contributions. The day the client dies, a large sum of tax-free dollars will be paid to the charity. Perhaps they'll put the client's name on a building or create a scholarship in the family name. What it does is create a legacy and provide perpetuity in the name of the client.

People want to be remembered. And so do you—by prospects, clients, individuals you meet at conferences, members of your community, and others. Investments can be made on all levels, starting with those you make in yourself.

Special Report:

5 Common Mistakes to Avoid—Plus 3 Tips to Close More Sales

Marvin H. Feldman, CLU, ChFC, RFC

You can't continue selling as you have been or you'll put yourself out of business. Our client and prospect base is changing rapidly. Social media, three-second attention spans and two generations who are growing up exclusively in a digital world have put an end to business as usual.

If you'd like to survive in this business, you'll need to adapt to the trends that are changing the way people buy. To do that, you'll need to stop making these (very!) common mistakes.

Mistake #1:
You're communicating with people the way you're comfortable with.

The average age of an insurance agent is 58. How close in age are you to that number? The closer the proximity, the higher the probability is that you're not getting your communications right. **It's time to rethink the "across the kitchen table" and "at my office" mindset,** and start communicating with clients and prospects how they'd prefer.

The "in person" or "over the phone" methods of outreach are quickly shifting. People are time-pressed and are looking for ways to connect that fit into their schedule, not the other way around. Just look at these numbers: for **those under age 45, more than half would prefer contact via email,** with 19% open to a video conference and 14% to getting their communications via text, according the 2014 Insurance Barometer Study by Life Happens and LIMRA. If communicating this way doesn't come naturally to you, then it's time to reach out and find someone to help you begin navigating these technologies.

Mistake #2:
You give them a solution before they understand they have a problem.

When we meet with a client or prospect, we often bring our enthusiasm to the table, but in the wrong way. You're excited about a new product you have for them and you promptly start a conversation launching into all its benefits. **The client or prospect is left dazed, not really understanding what has just happened** and how you can actually help them. And ultimately they don't end up acting on your advice. Sound familiar?

Telling them about a product first isn't going to work, because they aren't looking for a solution— they don't even know they have a problem. **You must first establish that there is a problem, a problem that you can help them solve with a product.** That brings me to the next mistake.

Mistake #3:
You avoid the risk portion of planning.

While you may be helping them grow their portfolios, have you also helped them understand what could happen to all that hard work and planning if something catastrophic were to happen? **Have you asked them the tough questions:** What if you were to die prematurely? What if you were injured and unable to work for a long period of time, or permanently? What if you lived too long?

Once you have established the fact that there would be a problem if one or more of these things happened, **then you can introduce your solution:** life, disability and/or long-term care insurance, that for pennies on the dollar will solve these problems for them.

Mistake #4:
You're using a "foreign" language.

Our industry is mired in technological terms. Terms like death benefit and premium are as ordinary to us as breathing, but most people aren't familiar with them. The LIMRA study "Get Real Already," found that nearly **three-quarters of people couldn't define "permanent life insurance" or "underwriting,"** while two-thirds were unsure of the terms "rider," "guarantees," "living benefit" or "annuity."

Did you know that there are nearly 19 million of what LIMRA calls "stuck shoppers" in the U.S.? These are people who understand the benefit of life insurance and are willing to buy, but have somehow gotten stuck in the buying process. LIMRA found that **a key factor in the stuck shopper dilemma was lack of clear and authentic communication.**

The bottom line is: They're not going to buy if they're not comfortable or if they don't understand what you're talking about. Instead, **use everyday language that puts your prospects at ease** and paints a positive picture for them. The LIMRA study says that doing so acts "as a confidence builder; and, as their confidence rises, their comfort level grows."

Mistake #5:
You turn a blind eye to social media.

You can come up with a hundred excuses why you don't need to be on or pay attention to social media, but with 2 billion people using these outlets—from Facebook to Twitter to LinkedIn—it just makes sense.

Social media can help you on two fronts: client retention and acquisition. First, it can help you strengthen the relationships you have with clients when you interact with them on these outlets—just view them as extensions of the communication tools you already use, like email and phone calls. In fact, 77% of respondents in an Accenture report ("How Tech-Savvy Advisors Can Regain Investor Trust") said that social media has helped them with client retention. In addition, 49% of advisors using social media acquired new clients that way (Putnam Investment Survey of Financial Advisors' Use of Social Media, 2013).

Life Happens is a great resource to rely on as you start or grow your social networks. It publishes more than 2,500 posts each year across all its networks. It's easy to follow Life Happens on its social properties and simply share what you think your friends and followers would like to see— instant content. In addition, Life Happens Pro has a comprehensive offering of social media content for you to use: graphics, statistics, prewritten posts, as well as some posts that have already gone viral.

Change is hard, there's no doubt about that. But if you want to grow your business and acquire new clients, you've got to **stop making the same mistakes over and over again.** Pick one of these and make the changes you need in order to put this mistake permanently behind you. Then, move on to the next.

But, PLEASE don't stop reading yet. I have 3 Tips to Help You Close More Sales.

We've just talked about how to make sure prospects show up at your doorstep (literal or digital!) and that they listen to what you have to say. But we also need to ensure that you turn those prospects into clients or that your clients are acting on your advice.

After more than 40 years in the business, I've learned a few lessons about closing sales. Here are three that are easy to implement.

 1. Commit to following up. This advice seems straightforward, but I see agents and advisors skip this step all the time. They send out large quantities of marketing emails or direct mail pieces to prospects and clients all at once. This is a waste of time and money. Honestly, how many good, long-term clients have you ever gotten from a direct mail piece or email that wasn't accompanied by a phone call? I'd guess zero.

The key is not to stop using this technique. Instead, **send out only enough solicitations that you can**

follow up with by phone. So, how many calls can you make in a week? Twenty or 25 perhaps? Then send out 20 or 25 pieces—and follow up!

2. Give them a clear choice. Ask them, **"Would you like to *go to* the bank or *be* the bank?"** Death brings about a lot of financial obligations and stresses, both short term and long term. From paying immediate funeral expenses to meeting ongoing bills, most American families will need a stream of income when a breadwinner—and often a stay-at-home parent—dies. The choice they have is clear: at that time of profound grief, they can choose to go to a bank to ask for the money they'll need, which must be paid back with interest, or they can choose to be the bank, by receiving the death benefit from a life insurance policy, which is theirs to keep and use as they wish and need.

If you're working with the middle market, **it's often a matter of choosing between relying on the charity of others**—donations and handouts from church, friends and family—**or having you, the agent, deliver the money** they need at the moment they need it most. Ask them which they'd prefer.

3. For business owners, ask to be put on their payroll. When you're helping business owners, you often have solutions, such as a buy/sell agreement, with a large premium attached to it. If the owner is balking at the premium, put it into context. Ask them, "How much do you pay the secretary or janitor or manager? Give me a number." After they have responded, ask, "If you had to hire one or more of these people, would it make a difference to your bottom line?"

The point of this line of questioning is to **help them understand that hiring those people is part of doing business**—they are there to solve a particular need. So, ask them to put you on the payroll as well. You can tell them, "The day one of the partners dies I'm going to walk in with $X million. That will allow you to buy out that share of the business, and the business is going to continue ..." **Remind them that the premium is not the problem, the premium is the solution to the problem.**

No doubt about it, these are tough conversations to have. But when you frame the conversation in a way that your prospects and clients know they have a problem, and that you have a solution they can buy for pennies on the dollar, then your job becomes a whole lot easier.

I'd love to hear your thoughts. You can contact me at **mfeldman@lifehappens.org.**

Marvin H. Feldman, CLU, ChFC, RFC, is president of the Feldman Financial Group in Palm Harbor, FL, and president and CEO of Life Happens in Arlington, VA. He is a 41-year Million Dollar Round Table member and was the 2002 president. He is a 33-year member of the MDRT Top of the Table and a past Top of the Table chairman. He also is the recipient of the 2011 John Newton Russell award, the highest honor bestowed on an individual by the insurance industry.

CHAPTER 4

You're Not Just Selling Insurance, You're Running a Business

Success is never owned. It is rented, and the rent is due every day.

As a new agent or advisor, the training you receive is typically not about running a business, which includes staff management, client relationships, and client retention. It instead focuses on cross-selling products—whole life, universal life, variable life, indexed life, critical care, long-term care, annuities, and mutual funds—all the different products the companies have to offer, and of course there are many. But while learning to sell these products is essential, so is running your business in a way that positions you for longevity. In short: **your business is your most important product**.

* * * *

STAFFING: AN IMPORTANT COMPONENT IN THE SUCCESS OR FAILURE OF YOUR BUSINESS

Some years ago, we wanted to find out if we could make our Ohio office more efficient and get more work out of the staff we had in place. We hired a firm that sent an efficiency expert to come in and do a full-scale assessment of everything, analyzing each employee in the process.

When the report came back, the comments were that they were amazed at how much work we were getting out of our staff. There was nothing we needed to do to make them more efficient.

But in the course of analyzing the company, the efficiency expert had asked that everyone take some time to write down their job description. Interestingly, this ended up working against us in the long run because, when we asked an employee to do something other than what they had written, the response would typically be, "But that's not in my job description." Somehow in the process of writing everything down, they'd pigeonholed themselves—kind of like a typecast actor who plays a curmudgeon or a mom or a detective so many times, they end up not playing anything else. In this case, our employees could not see themselves as anything but the character in their job description.

In business, however, employees need to understand that their job really is whatever they're asked to do (within reason, of course). **I always said, you hire for ability; you fire for negative attitude.** And while you certainly don't have a crystal ball, learning to ascertain at a hiring interview who is a team player and who isn't will serve you well, saving you headaches down the line.

Part of being a team player is understanding that, while office politics are unavoidable, **being able to subordinate politics to the task at hand is priority one.** Office cohesion is key.

Years ago, we had an employee who took particular delight in regaling others with different versions of a story or incident, causing whatever kind of division and outright mayhem she could by stirring up their reactions. Warnings meant nothing to her, and in time we let her go because she was not part of the team as we needed it. Some degree of independence is certainly warranted in an office setting, as is creativity and initiative, but certainly not when it is used to under-mine the office's functionality as a whole.

Employees you hire have to understand from day one that the life insurance industry really isn't a nine-to-five job. There may be some days when they may be asked to report to work at 7:30 a.m., or stay until seven or eight at night to finish preparing a major presentation that, without them working together, would not get out the door. Billionaire businessman and Dallas Mavericks owner Mark Cuban said it best: "Treat your customers like they own you, because they do." If an employee does not endorse that concept, they have no business working for *your* business. But it is not all business all the time. Some-times I give my staff an extra day off just because I can, and this can pay extra dividends when you need that extra effort from your team.

So what are the fundamentals of running a business centered on selling life insurance and related products and services?

Personnel-wise, you look for people who work well together, who exercise good judgment, and who have the ability to make decisions. While it may not be incumbent upon someone hired to do filing to make pivotal decisions on a daily basis, if you are looking to grow and promote from within, a spark of ambition is a good thing. **This kind of hiring is a form of insurance in itself, because the constant replacement of employees is a time- and energy-consuming task.**

There is also an adage about being happy in life that talks about marrying well, marrying someone who is positive, supportive, and shares your values. Similarly, hiring a competent office manager or personal assistant whom you can count on to take care of things exactly as you would, especially when you're not there, is a key ingredient in a well-run office.

To empower your staff, it is also important to know how to dele-gate responsibility. It's crucial to give appropriate staff the authority and latitude to make decisions. And while delegating is not letting go completely, it is training for the day when an individual can make decisions independently, requiring less of your time. Naturally, there are scenarios in which you want to maintain control, and on those occasions you want your staff to report back to you and say, "Here's what happened, and here's where you need to make some decisions." But in more routine matters, give them authority and delegate.

Along the way, **employees need to be acknowledged** for the effort they make, for what they do well. They need to feel valued.

Some employers like to pay performance bonuses and some don't. It depends on the precedent you want to set within your organization. At times I've found bonuses to be a problem. Even if you've always set goals and achieved them, and have paid bonuses accordingly, there is going to be a point in time when because of an illness (yours or a close family member's), a downturn in the business, or something else unexpected, you may not make your goal. The only time our office did not make its goals was the year my mother passed away. My father had spent so much time caring for her during her illness that for the first time, office goals were not met, bonuses could not be issued, and the staff was unhappy. After that, we decided to approach performance rewards in a different way.

You have to be very careful when designing your compensation systems that you don't paint yourself into a corner. My take on performance bonuses is that they should be individually directed to those who achieve specific goals. In my practice, though, largely as a result of this experience, we stopped paying performance bonuses and instead raised everybody's salaries.

We also established interim goals and rewards throughout the year, perhaps a trip to New York City for the weekend, and some specific goals for certain employees, but bonuses were no longer expected automatically.

Early on, I talked about the individual who was hired to do my cold-calling. She received an hourly wage, and each time she set an appointment that was kept, she got an additional sum of money. If that case went on to become a client, she received a small percentage of the commissions. She had great incentive all along to work hard in order to see things through to the end, without the promise of a big, separate bonus at the end of the year.

You will need to address bonuses as you add staff and determine the compensation system which will work for you. I know many agents and advisors who do not believe in bonuses, but bonuses are an excellent method of acknowledging an employee's performance and awarding them accordingly.

* * *

CLIENT CLARITY AND TRAINING

In addition to highly dependable staff, taking the time to train clients from the outset about how they're going to be serviced by that staff is vital to running an efficient business. In this manner, they know immediately how things work and what to expect, minimizing any time you might have to spend explaining things to a client who thinks they are suddenly being managed by someone other than you. No one likes to feel handed off, and proper planning, execution, and communication of protocol can prevent that feeling from arising.

There were times when clients who were being managed by my staff, and not by me directly, called me anyway. In training these clients, I may have failed to impress upon them that if they contacted me, I'd be referring them back to the specific staff member assigned to their case, who is intimately familiar with the details and has likely already had contact with them. In time, they usually came to understand and even appreciate our office protocol.

• • • •

BUDGET GUIDELINES

Business owners know that income ebbs and flows. In my practice, income could arrive in large sums or it might be two, three, four, or five months before we'd see anything significant. Our cash flow was not level and consistent. Whether your office is large or small, everything hinges on what you're doing, how you're doing it, what the commission levels are, when they come in, and much more. In short, budgeting well is key, and paramount to that is having ready sources of cash. Your operating expenses will continue even though your income may vary from month to month.

Those sources can take the form of money that's earmarked (for emergencies, for example) and set aside in bank accounts, CDs or other investments, or a line of credit that may be backed up by these investments. Perhaps you've invested in a life insurance policy from which you can borrow or use as collateral for a line of credit. For loans, the bank wants to be assured it will get its money back, and by taking these steps, you're ensuring that it will.

I worked on very complicated cases involving sophisticated estate planning, business succession planning, and buy-sell agreements, where I had to bring in multiple outside experts. And if there were multiple business partners, each had to bring in an attorney. The way I functioned was essentially as the facilitator, or the quarterback, to make sure everything got done. Despite the fact that the paperwork for the insurance and underwriting may have been in place practically from the beginning, and policies were ready to issue, nothing moved until legal affairs and documents were in order, which could take months. Again, having a budget and interim sources of money on hand was essential.

* * * *

GENERATING BUSINESS

Part of running a business is generating business. In that respect, prospecting is a priority. Many people use social settings like golf, tennis, cocktail parties, professional organizations, and the like for prospecting, and it seems to work well, though I was never comfortable with it. Everyone needs to work where they are comfortable, which for me was an office or perhaps a restaurant over lunch or a cup of coffee.

Previously I talked about the value of investing in seminars and conferences that help you expand your thinking, methodology, and expertise. I can honestly say I've gotten just as much out of talking with attendees who were there for similar purposes. This may also generate business for you because, just as attendees may become the experts you turn to in order to help secure clients, you have the opportunity to become the expert they need in light of your own specialty.

* * * *

THE CHINA EGG

At first glance, you may think a "china egg" is a client who requires special handling—as the expression goes, "with kid gloves." Actually, though, just as a china egg doesn't hatch, there are instances when you may have a prospect in your system for months or years who never becomes a client. In trying to build a business, you may hold onto people for long periods of time, scheduling more calls, more in-person presentations, whatever it takes; but good business practices warrant jettisoning them from your system eventually so you are not drowning in inactive scenarios.

It used to be we had prospects written out on three-by-five index cards, piled on our desks. By the time those cards turned yellow, it was time to throw them out. Technology has made that process more efficient. Now there's a name and a growing amount of information in your client-management system, and maybe even reminders that pop up. But after a certain point, it's time to purge. It may be prudent to keep them on your mailing list—my office sometimes did unusual mailings such as Halloween cards to engage prospects and keep us in clients' orbit—but nothing more. Sometimes people shy away from purging because the sheer number of prospects on their list gives them confidence that they have people to call on. To keep your business running efficiently, however, staying current with your client and prospect list is the only way to go.

* * * *

EYE ON THE BALL

Finally, in running a lean, efficient, responsive, and successful business, it's essential to maintain your focus. It may be natural to want to extend your reach and become proficient in everything—all manner of products and expertise. But while you and your business can attempt to do everything, you can't do everything well. **Choose where you want to spend your time, effort, and money, and develop your staff expertise there, bringing in outside experts when necessary to handle the rest.** And remember that building and running a business takes time and practice to get it right. You must be willing to fail in order to succeed. **Failing is not failure unless you fail to try again.**

CHAPTER 5

The World Accepts Generalists, but It Embraces Team Leaders

We are in a noble profession. We need to be proud
of what we do and how we do it.

My specialty has always been estate planning, along with business succession planning. I spent time in money management and offered investment advice over the years to many clients, but that wasn't really my area of expertise. When I needed knowledge and proficiency in something else to court a client, I added someone to my team who fit the bill, often from the outside knowing I'd have to share the commission. But without the other expert, there may have been no commission in the first place. It's like the adage "part of something is better than all of nothing." In the movie *Wall Street,* Gordon Gekko famously says, "Greed is good." He says it in the context of motivation and risk taking, but a good team leader recognizes that this isn't always the case. **In fact, greed can cause you to lose the client.**

Of course, you want to maintain control of the client as much as possible. It can be difficult to give up any of that power, understanding that you are going to have to trust someone else to provide the right information and make appropriate recommendations. You can try to do it alone and recommend something that may generate more in the way of commissions, or allow you to keep the entire commission, but you always want to do the right thing for the client. What you do or don't do for a client will come back to you in the end, good or bad.

The challenge in estate planning and business succession planning is that, in many cases, the client doesn't understand the extent of their financial responsibility or the range of possible problems and conditions. There are complicated issues to deal with in estate planning—estate liquidity, legacy planning, charitable bequests, and more. When you bring in succession planning, you've got multiple family members involved in the business, multiple family members outside of the businesses, questions about how to treat everybody equitably. Someone might say, "I like you, Paul, but if something happens to you, I don't want to be in partnership with your wife running the business, so we need to arrange an equitable buyout for your share."

There are so many scenarios that people don't really contemplate because they are uncomfortable confronting them. As someone who has chosen to specialize in this area, it's my job to use my expertise to walk them through issues, help them overcome hurdles they may encounter, guide them in the decision-making process, and bring everything to an optimal conclusion.

But again, not every prospect of mine was interested in estate planning or business succession planning, so as a team leader I cultivated a network of financial industry professionals, attorneys, and CPAs who concentrated on pension planning, health or disability insurance, income planning, stock purchase arrangements, and other specialty areas.

In Chapter 2 I talked about harnessing outside experts to help deliver the client when what you know isn't quite enough or your expertize is in the wrong area. As a team leader, your vision comes into play when you recognize what's needed, anticipate what else may be needed, acknowledge that you may not be able to provide this to the extent it's needed, and then work hard to assemble a solid team to respond to all scenarios and contingencies. It's about knowing where to go, when to go, and to whom to go. If you have a kidney issue, your primary care physician sends you to a nephrologist; if you have heart problems, you are directed to a cardiologist. It is the same with teams in the life insurance and financial services industry where we bring in outside specialists.

If you're new to the business, chances are you're working with a specific company that is providing the training and/or you have a mentor giving you a lot of input. **I have always believed mentors are vital for success in our business. A good mentor will help you get to the next level.** This is where you have the opportunity to learn from others' experience—and mistakes—so you don't have to expend a lot of time and energy trying to do it all by yourself. It's really a matter of asking the right questions.

When I was growing up, I had a sign in my room that said, "Please, I would rather make my own mistakes." Now that I am a little older and wiser, I know the importance of learning from others' mistakes, because I can't possibly live long enough to make them all myself. And I don't have the time! Neither do you.

Learn from other agents, managers, and mentors when and how to bring in experts, or pick up the phone and call someone you've met in your professional travels and say, "I need something here. I have this particular issue with a prospect or client. Do you know whom I can contact?" One of the great things about our industry is that people want the best for you and are willing to share their knowledge to make sure you get it. **I have always said that early in your career, you don't know what you don't know. Better to avail yourself of all the human resources around you so that you continuously learn**

more; at the same time, understand that you can't know or do it all.

In your first several years in the life insurance and financial services industry, being a generalist is probably all you can be until you develop expertise to specialize in an area that appeals to you. The team leadership skills you develop will enable you to better serve and expand your client base. In essence, revenue you generate will be exceeding what's possible with a more limited practice.

* * * *

BUILDING THE TEAM

Attending seminars and conferences is a way of learning all you can about this industry as well as adjunct industries and professions. I've found that people entering the business today are less likely to go out and join groups, even though this effort may connect them with experts who can help them expand their business. At the same time, the more you reach out, the more you improve your chances of being engaged yourself by other businesses as a team specialist in your area of expertise.

I used an attorney from a particular law firm to consult on cases from time to time. One day I received a call that his firm was doing some estate planning for an individual with very high net worth. The attorney wanted me to spearhead the research and design a solution. There were probably 10 to 15 other agents vying for this opportunity, but the firm knew me well. They knew the quality of my work and were confident I would recommend only what was appropriate for the client. It was a very complicated estate planning case with multiple family members involved. The end result was that we wrote an exceptionally large case with a premium of more than seven figures.

In time, we also did a great deal of work for other fam
for whom we wrote a tremendous amount of life insura......

You might say there was some team leader reciprocity going on
here, and there are many dozens of examples from my practice where
knowing whom to call and trust made acquiring and servicing clients
possible.

* * * *

On a more fundamental level, while being a strong team leader is
about knowing who can help, and when to bring them in, leading is
also about sending the right message to the team you already have
in place or that you are building: your day-to-day staff. In theory, my
formula is simple, though in practice it takes discipline and commitment in order to work.

Over the years, I have found the following concepts to be integral
to my team's effectiveness, and made a point to affirm them whenever
I could. I may repeat them a time or two throughout this book, but
only to reinforce how vital they are to success in this industry:

- **Prioritize and focus on first things first, because life rewards action.**

- **Every problem in our industry has a solution, and every solution is an opportunity. The price tag for the solution may be as simple as paying the premium on the policy.**

- **Life is about helping others. It is not about you or me. If you are lucky, you find a career that brings meaning to your life.**

- Do what you do best and delegate the rest. That's called efficiency.

- Simplify your life. Most stuff just doesn't matter. Eliminate the unnecessary and the unimportant. Concentrate on the significant.

- You must be willing to fail in order to succeed. Failing is not failure unless you fail to try again.

- Always finish what you start; don't procrastinate. Ask the question, "What is my number-one priority right now?" Then do it!

- Success is never owned. It is rented, and the rent is due every day.

- Successful people do what others won't.

- Leaders are expected to work longer, harder, and smarter.

- Experience is the name everyone gives to their mistakes, so learn from the mistakes of others because you can't possibly live long enough to make them all yourself.

- Establish goals, priorities, and deadlines. Planning produces profits.

- A professional is someone who performs at their best when they feel like it the least.

- Develop a positive attitude. The biggest asset you have is your earning capacity, and that depends entirely on your attitude.

- **Be dissatisfied.** The feeling of having done a job well is rewarding, but the desire to do it better will make you stronger and more effective at what you do.

- **Develop your potential.** You mold your character and future by your thoughts and actions. Reaching beyond your comfort zone develops your potential, and passion prompts you to set—and reach—higher goals.

CHAPTER 6

The Problem Is the Problem; the Premium Is the Solution—Not the Problem!

People may tell you they have enough money to last the rest of their lives, and that may be true unless they buy something.

The life insurance and financial services industry is about protecting tomorrow, the what ifs. As an agent or advisor, to a large extent it's up to you to help determine exactly what tomorrow will look like for each client. This is based on resolving a problem they have today, **especially because they may not understand they even have a problem until you reveal it to them.**

Sometimes in our industry, agents and advisors look at the premium as the problem because they're concerned about how the client is going to be able to write the check. But the premium is not the problem: **it's the solution to the problem.** Without it, the problem doesn't go away and can, in fact, eventually destroy a company, its employees, and its heirs.

So how do we get to the solution?

In five decades in this industry, I'm unable to count the number of times I've gone into a meeting with a prospect whose needs I believed

I'd thoroughly researched in advance, thinking I was there to explain estate planning, or perhaps business or financial planning, only to end up on another topic entirely. By asking a specific series of questions and reading between the lines, and then asking and listening some more, I ascertained that the prospect had other more pressing needs than I had thought. Consequently, the products and services I was ready to offer would not have solved the problem at all. I had to be prepared to change direction, to reconfigure and pivot 90 degrees or maybe even 180 degrees, to find the right solution.

The fact is, in these situations I may not have acquired the client at all had I not made a continuous effort to develop a powerful set of listening skills. **The kinds of questions I knew to ask and how to ask them** were what led to solutions in these scenarios. There's debate about who actually said it, with some attributing it to Voltaire, but it is absolutely true that "it's not the answers you give, but the questions you ask." Our industry underscores that premise. **Real success is invariably based on asking the right questions.**

Many times I've been called in as an outside expert by an agent to attend a client meeting, and I quickly realized the agent just wasn't listening to what the client was saying and was poised to lose out. Homing in on the real issue, the one which the client may not even be aware of, and shifting their attention accordingly, is the key to finding the right solution. But there is both a psychology and an art to doing this well.

So what are they?

First, it's no secret that as a rule people like to talk about themselves. I've been in meetings with total strangers who, with very little encouragement, opened up their personal, family, business, and financial lives to me. On the other hand, at a prospect meeting, you may find someone who borders on being curt, looking at their watch and saying they agreed to give you 20 minutes, so what exactly is it you have say? But if you've invested time and practice in learning precisely what questions to ask, and how to listen, even this kind of scenario can yield surprising results.

If you are meeting at someone's home or office, there are bound to be photographs, plaques, trophies, citations, art, awards—even a favorite old piece of sports equipment or memorabilia—any of which make for a great place to start the conversation, and which can reveal more about the prospect's needs and wants than a formal inquiry.

I've always been called a "gearhead." I love anything with speed, cars or otherwise, and my wife is exactly the same way. This is what motivated her to learn to fly and spend a number of years as my corporate pilot. I tend to channel my passion and propensity for speed into more earthbound pursuits, like automotive racing and sports cars. If I found evidence that a prospect or client was also inclined that way (and many of them were), it served as common ground on which to build. Over time, it would get to the point where they'd take the reins early on in a meeting and ask, "So, Marv, what on Earth are you driving now?" It was always a great, lighthearted exchange and provided a smooth transition into the business at hand.

With a prospect, or a client to whom you are looking to add products and services, you need to take the time to learn to converse about all kinds of things that may be of interest to them. You don't have to be a master of all, just know enough to engage in easy, comfortable, feel-good conversation. The great author and poet Maya Angelou once said that while people may not always remember what you said, or what you did, they will always remember how you made them feel. Take that sage observation into your business meetings and watch what happens.

Ask questions about items you may observe in a prospect's home or office, listen carefully to the way in which they answer, and continue to probe in a genuinely interested, nonthreatening way. In this way, you will learn a great deal and begin to earn the prospect's trust and respect.

It's important to know how to ask questions that cannot be answered by a simple yes or no, because that's the end of the discussion. You want to ask open-ended questions that cause people to think and reflect, and require more of an explanation on their part: the who, what, when, where, and why questions.

To help streamline the process, I have put together a list of more than 100 questions categorized by family and life issues, business issues, life insurance, investing, financial focus, and long-term care insurance, including long-term care power phrases that will help you respond to the toughest client questions about why that kind of insurance is important. They are at the end of this chapter, and they are the summation of almost 50 years of experience. This work has the potential to save you decades of figuring these things out for yourself and making mistakes that can result in a loss of business along the way. As with most anything else, studying and practicing these questions, putting them into your own words, and making the whole process so comfortable it becomes second nature will determine how far you can go in your insurance and financial services industry career.

• • • •

When it comes to learning, you should always be a student of the industry, something I address in depth in Chapter 10. A lot of people, including Steve Jobs, have encouraged those around them to "stay hungry," something with which I wholeheartedly concur. It will distinguish you in the financial services field, and in fact can be the difference between an average career and one that is stratospheric in terms of achievement. To help achieve this, I highly recommend relying on managers, mentors, and certainly this book as an educational tool along with everything else you can learn on your own. In this manner, focusing your time and energy on what I call "getting ready to get ready," you will find your way more quickly. Clearly, preparation is paramount in achieving and exceeding your goals in this industry.

I strongly advocate taking notes when talking with clients and prospects. In addition to chronicling every thought, statement, response, and more, as people tend to have "selective memory," note taking gives the impression that you are truly interested—truly *invested* in the outcome. It is also a tool to create the perception that your work is meticulous, which of course it must be to scale the heights in this industry. You may prefer to leave a meeting, get to your vehicle, and immediately dictate everything you discussed into a recording device rather than relying on notes, which may turn out to be incomplete (not all of us are gifted transcribers!). But again, sitting with a client and taking notes underscores that what the prospect or client says has real merit and that you don't want to miss anything.

In the process of gaining someone's confidence through all of this, you're going to discover what their "hot buttons" are: what is of the most concern to them today. Then you'll be able to recommend truly precise solutions for the future.

Since I am a specialist in business and estate planning, an agent brought me into a case because the client needed some help in those areas. As always, I started asking what I assumed were relevant questions. Within a few minutes I'd determined that he was not at all interested in either business or estate planning. Because this process becomes a matter of course as you get better and better at what you do, based on his responses, I was able to transition to inquiring about his company's pension plan by asking if he was maxing out his pension benefits and shifting the client's thinking in the process. While he was putting in as much money as the law allowed, he was quite concerned about retirement planning and desired to put in more, but he had no idea there was a way to do it. I knew there was and redirected him to a separate pension-type program, using a life insurance product (something like a Roth IRA, but life insurance) that could accommodate unlimited funding, providing a tax-free income stream down the road.

As it turned out, the client had an additional $40,000 to $50,000 a year to invest in a Supplemental Life Insurance Retirement Program, or maximum-funded life insurance policy. This product could be funded up to the permissible amount and even overfunded, though the client could run into some tax issues, so we were careful not to do that. Because he had 15 to 20 years for the product to work, this was a highly viable solution to the client's problem, a problem that was not anticipated going in but that my series of questions had revealed. Had I not developed these questions, and over time studied, practiced, honed, and become entirely comfortable asking them, the agent and I may have left that meeting without writing a policy.

Another prospect of mine was a highly successful family-run dairy in the Midwest. I'd done some research on this prospect and had sent the pre-approach letter and made the phone call myself, believing this was probably the perfect scenario for some extensive estate planning.

During the meeting, as I began asking questions, it was readily apparent that there were some interfamily problems. There were those who worked hard, wanted the business to grow, were earning a salary, and wanted to reinvest the profits in the dairy. Then there was a whole other set of family members who were not active in the dairy, who took dividends from it but didn't want any capital put back in. They just wanted the money. Ultimately, there was no policy written because the family members couldn't even agree on what needed to be done from a life insurance perspective to protect everybody. What they needed was more in the realm of family counseling.

You don't get to solve every issue or write every policy, but by asking the right questions, I realized the need to equalize funding for family members was far more pressing than any kind of estate or business succession planning.

In many family businesses, there are various family members in and out of the business. So how do you equalize the value to the surviving heirs? You can't just give the business to the working heirs, because that's the bulk of the estate. So what can be done for the others? It's called **Estate Equalization.**

Here's the magic of life insurance: if a business's valuation is at $5 million, you give that to the heirs who are working in the business. Then you purchase a $5 million block of life insurance for those family members who are not in the business. Both groups of individuals end up with the same amount of money. Everything is equalized for pennies on the dollar, the price of the premium compared to the price of the problem. You haven't had to destroy a company or give out stock to family members who are not active in the business and have no interest in having it grow, expand, and succeed into the third generation. The questions listed at the end of this chapter are the kinds of questions that will get you to the right solution, but they need to be posed in the most unaggressive way so that the prospect feels comfortable opening up.

◦ ◦ ◦ ◦

One of the tools that helped me present ideas to prospects and clients so that they had a clear understanding of what I could do for them do was the flow chart. The flow chart is an important visual aid that worked well for me as it elicited a great response which in turn allowed me to ask the most relevant questions in search of the right solution.

Developed by a member of my study group, which we will talk about in Chapter 10, the flow chart not only incorporated the products and services my office provided but illustrated scenarios, such as pension planning, disability insurance, and group insurance, where I would bring in an outside expert. In this regard, the prospect or client was assured that all the bases would be covered. It was an integral part of my practice for more than 30 years and I am certain helped turn **a suspect into a prospect into a client** more times than I can recall.

This flow chart worked very much like a sales track, allowing me to read the chart with my prospect to determine which specific area was the prospect's hot button. The question to ask the prospect after reviewing the chart is, "Mr. Prospect, of everything we have discussed, which is of most concern to you today?" Then it is time to stop, listen to the prospect's response, and frame your next questions based on what the prospect is telling you.

With all of these techniques, when all is said and done, the prospect or client is going to come to the conclusion that you are someone they can trust—someone who is going to do the best job for them, their business, their partners, and their family for the long haul. I've even found that over time, the relationship becomes so sound, clients call seeking advice for matters that may be unrelated to the financial services industry because they value my judgment. Quite simply, I've earned their trust.

Feldman Financial Group

How much of what you own is really yours?

* Analysis   * Implementation
* Design   * Monitoring

Wealth Preservation

* Estate Planning
* Buy – Sell Funding
* Stock Redemptions
* Key Management Insurance
* Personal Insurance
* Charitable Trusts
* Critical Illness Protection

Employee Benefits

* Non-Qualified Pension Plans
* Qualified Retirement Plans
* Deferred Compensation
  Plans
* Group Medical, Life and
  Disability
* Salary Continuation Plans

Investments

* IRA Accounts
* Tax Deferred Annuities
* Mutual Funds
* Limited Partnerships
* Stocks & Bonds
* Personal Financial Plan
  Compliance disclosure required.

Consulting

We help you keep together what you've worked so hard to put together.

QUESTIONS FOR PROSPECTS AND CLIENTS

Success lies not in the answers you give,
but the questions you ask.
—Socrates

QUESTIONS FOR "FAMILY & LIFE ISSUES"

- When was the last time someone, not involved in your planning, gave you a second opinion as to whether or not you have covered all the bases?

- Do you have enough confidence in your advisors to let me give you a second opinion?

- What do you want to accomplish with your life? Why are you here? What is your purpose?

- What are your key concerns?

- What does financial security mean to you?

- What does financial freedom mean to you?

- What do you want to accomplish with your money?

- What is your family financial philosophy?

- What's important about money to you?

- What is your overall financial and investment strategy or game plan?

- What are your goals?

- What is your exit strategy?

- How and when do you see yourself retiring? What will you do, and what will it cost you to do it—not just the day after you retire, but 10,20 and even 30 years later?

- Where do you want your money to go?

- How do you want to be remembered by your children, your grandchildren, your favorite charities, your community, and society?

- Is there an institution that you care deeply about, a church, charity or school to which you would wish to leave a meaningful legacy, assuming we could create a highly tax efficient way for you to do so?

- If you had a family foundation, what would you want it to be known for?

- What would you like your ideal calendar to look like in five years?

- If you know with virtual certainty that you were going to die within the next six months, what changes would you make in your life and in your planning?

- What changes would you like to make in your overall financial situation?

- How do you feel about the income tax system in this country?

- How do you feel about estate taxes and related costs?

- Could your children pay the estate tax in the next nine months without liquidating key assets?

- Assuming, as we have to do, that when you are both gone, up to half your estate will get taxed away, how do you want the tax to be paid? If you want your children to just pay the half, might they be forced to sell something you really wouldn't want them to have to sell?

- What is an acceptable amount of estate tax shrinkage? What have you done to get there?

- What have you done to protect your assets from divorce, bankruptcy or creditors of your children?

- Are your parents living, and if so, will you be expected to contribute to their support at some point?

- Have you made provisions for the possibility that you may need nursing home or other care late in your life?

- What are your thoughts about "The American Dream?"

- What is your understanding of "The American Dream?"

- What are your thoughts about giving your children a headstart?

- What are your thoughts about inherited wealth?

- What concerns do you have regarding your children and inherited wealth?

- To whom would your spouse or your children turn for advice on managing their inheritance?

QUESTIONS FOR "BUSINESS ISSUES"

- What is your exit strategy from your business?

- If your business had to be sold after your death or disability, could it be sold for a profit?

- Who will own your business when you retire or die?

- Who will control your business when you retire or die?

- Who will run your business when you retire or die?

- Do you want your spouse to have control after your death?

- Do you have a salary continuation agreement with your company?

- To what extent will your family be involved in your business in the future?

- Do you want your business to be divided among your family equally or just those who are in the business? What about family outside the business?

- What are you doing to recruit, retain, and reward key people in your business?

- Which employees are critical to the success of the company?

- What are your key concerns about your business?

- Would your creditors be nervous if you became disabled or died?

- Who do you owe? Could you pay them back in the next 10 minutes?

- Have you established a business continuation plan? Is it documented? Does it provide for a mandatory buy-out or a right of first refusal? Is it adequately funded?

QUESTIONS ABOUT "LIFE INSURANCE"

- Most people do not seem to understand life insurance very well. Tell me, what do you know about life insurance?

- What is your philosophy regarding life insurance?

- What financial formula did you use to determine how much life insurance to buy?

- What prompted your most recent purchase of life insurance?

- How did you choose the company that you purchased life insurance from?

- How did you select the agent?

- What are your thoughts regarding term insurance and cash value life insurance?

- If you were going to buy life insurance in the future, why would you buy it?

- How do you feel about life insurance on your spouse?

- How do you feel about life insurance on your children?

QUESTIONS ABOUT "INVESTING"

- What is your investment philosophy?

- What is your investment strategy?

- What results have you had with your investments over the past few years?

- What provisions have you made to have your retirement nest egg outpace inflation?

- What have you done to guarantee against the loss of your principal during retirement?

- How have you measured your results?

- To what extent have you relied on the advice of others regarding your investments?

- What would you have done differently regarding your investments?

- What role does diversification play in your investment planning?

- What types of investments do you prefer?

- How much time do you want to spend selecting and managing your investments?

- What is your exit strategy from your investments?

FINANCIAL FOCUS

- What role does money play in your life? What's important about money to you?

- What are your plans regarding retirement? What are you doing to accomplish your plans?

- What types of investments do you favor? Why?

- What are your investment results over the past five years? Are you pleased?

- Would you be pleased with the same results over the next five years? What would you do differently?

- How much time do you spend selecting and managing your investments? How much is your time worth?

- Do you feel you can outperform someone who spends all of his or her time managing investments?

- What would happen to you and your family if your income were to stop today?

- What have you done to enable your family to have an adequate income in the event of your death?

- Have you provided a cash cushion for emergencies, education funding, etc.?

- What role does life insurance play in your financial plans, both personally and in your business?

- How much life insurance do you have? How did you decide on that amount?

- To what extent are your spouse and children involved in your financial decision making?

- What advisors do you use and to what extent?

- How did you get started in your business?

- What makes your business different from the competition? What problems do you foresee?

- What are your plans for your business at your retirement or death or disability?

- What steps have you taken to accomplish your plans for your business?

- To what extent are your children involved in your business?

- Who will ultimately run your business? What are you doing to retain and reward them?

- What are you doing in terms of selective compensation plans for yourself and your key people?

- What impact would the loss of key people have on sales, profits, lines of credit, retirement plans, and stock value?

- How much vacation do you take? What if you were to go on vacation and not return?

- Where do you want your money to go?

- How do you feel about your children receiving a large inheritance? Why?

- When did you last update your will(s) and trust(s)?

- What is the approximate value of your estate?

- What is the potential estate tax impact and what have you done about it? How will the estate taxes be paid?

- To what extent have you made gifts to your children or considered doing so?

- What are your thoughts regarding giving or leaving assets to a favorite charity or to your community?

- If you knew you only had six months to live, what changes would you make? What if you had died last week?

- How do you want to be remembered by your children? Grandchildren? Employees? Community?

- What are your primary concerns and goals and why? What's really important to you?

- What would you like to accomplish as a result of our discussions? Who else should be involved?

- If you knew with virtual certainty that you were going to die within the next six months, what changes would you make in your life and in your planning?

KEY QUESTIONS AND POWER PHRASES
FOR LONG TERM CARE INSURANCE

- What do you think about when you hear the words long-term care?

- What are your questions and concerns about long-term care?

- Do you know or have you had experiences with someone who became frail or needed long-term care?

- What does your money mean to you?

- How concerned are you that a chronic illness will threaten your ability to continue to provide for your spouse?

- If you are in a second marriage, how important is it to distribute your assets to your children according to your prenuptial agreement or will?

- If there are not enough funds to pay for care, your spouse may be forced to use his or hers. My experience tells me that your children may be concerned about this.

- Long-term care insurance acts as a firewall; it allows the couple's agreement to keep assets separate during their lives to execute properly.

- Do you have a continuing financial obligation to any of your children or grandchildren that have personal problems or are physically or mentally challenged?

- If you live a long life and need care, what is your plan?

- What impact do you think long-term care will have on your family?

- Have you discussed the plan of long-term care with your children?

LTCi POWER PHRASES:

- Living a long life is very likely in your future. Planning for it now is a necessity. When you don't die, you live.

- When you live, you get old.

- When you get old, you may get frail or sick.

- When you get sick, you need care.

- And when you need care, care will cost money.

- I need to talk to you about the consequences your needing care will have on your family in your retirement portfolio.

- You may never get sick and need long-term care, but the consequences to your family and retirement portfolio could be so catastrophic that subject must at least be discussed.

- You're right. The chances of ending up in a nursing home are remote, but don't confuse that with growing old and needing some level of care, even at home.

- People don't go to nursing homes when they should. They go when the caregiver no longer has the physical or mental capacity to provide the care.

- The problem is not long-term care insurance, its long-term care <u>planning</u>.

- Long-term care insurance allows your retirement portfolio to perform for the purposes it was intended: retirement, not paying for care.

- Long-term care insurance does not replace what families do. It allows them to provide care longer and better.

- My clients don't purchase long-term care insurance to protect assets, they have choices to remain independent. They purchased long-term care insurance because they care for their family. They understand that even though they may never need care, the consequences to their family and retirement portfolio will be so severe, they must take action to protect both.

- Myths: Long-term care insurance protects the individual. Reality: Long-term care insurance protects the individual's family. Myth: Long-term care insurance protects assets. Reality: Long-term care insurance protects income stream.

- Mr. Client, I understand that your lifestyle will be supported by income generated from your investments and pensions. In fact, just about every dollar has been allocated for your retirement. The problem is that should you need care, you can't be assured that there will be sufficient income to support your lifestyle and pay for your spouse's care at the same time.

- If someone asks you to send them something in the mail, why not send them a list of some of your favorite questions? If you are trying to meet someone but are having trouble connecting with them, why not get permission from the individual or his or her assistant to snail mail or email them a few questions? What do you have to lose? And if they say their advisers have completed all the planning; ask if they have enough confidence in their adviser to allow you to give them a second opinion.

—*Provided by Howard Wight and Marvin H. Feldman*

CHAPTER 7

The Premium May Be a Bigger Deal for You Than for the Client

You need to fund a long-term problem with a long-term solution. The question is not at what age does the client want to retire, but at what income.

Some years ago, I was called in as an expert by a law firm in Pittsburgh to make a presentation to one of their clients. My solution to the client's problem was accepted, yet I can recall my level of discomfort the day I went back to collect the $1 million premium check. Despite the fact that they had understood the problem and accepted the solution, I was still uncomfortable. In fact, that day I'd rather have stayed at my desk all day drinking cold coffee and making cold calls, which you know are next to impossible for me. Well, not really. But I was concerned because they may have changed their mind! It was a bigger problem in my mind than it was in theirs.

When I arrived at the place of business, the CFO handed me the check, and I was out the door. It happened that quickly. So it was apparently not a big deal in anybody's mind but mine. Psychologically,

I really had to prepare myself to stand there, ask for, and accept the check, though I'd already been in the industry for a very long time. As appropriate as the astronomical premium was to the solution, the fact is those types of checks do not occur every day. It doesn't matter if a check is for $50,000 or $1 million, it's the right economic solution at the right time for that particular client.

When it comes to money, people clearly have different comfort levels. First, socioeconomic level can correspond to one's capacity for broaching the subject. Next, it's about the *perception* of what one feels is a reasonable amount to ask for given a particular situation. So if you're earning $50,000 or $100,000 a year, and you're talking to a prospect or client where their needs require $1 million or $10 million of death benefit with a $20,000 or $200,000 premium, it may be difficult for you to present and ask for the big numbers. But those kinds of numbers are what the prospect or client may consider normal, everyday checks when it comes to their business. It doesn't matter if you're talking about life insurance or financial services, or selling tractors, trucks, or anything else. It's what they need. If you're accustomed to selling one truck a day and suddenly you've got someone who needs 25 trucks, the check that they write to you is going to be 25 times the typical amount, and that's something they're prepared to write. **Think big. Be prepared to add the zero to both the problem and the solution.**

· · · ·

One of the things I've found extremely helpful in overcoming reluctance in asking for large sums of money is preparation, including practice. When I've had to present a speech, often someone will come up to me afterward to remark that I'm a natural speaker, how calm and relaxed I am, and how effortless it all looked. But what they don't see are the hours and hours and still more hours of preparation that went into making that presentation. I've diligently researched, studied, written, edited, practiced, refined, and practiced some more. As a result, it all comes across smoothly, I don't stumble on the words, and I don't hesitate by using a lot of "ahs" and "ums." I am also ready for any objections or challenges to what I'm presenting, prepared to respond in the most informed, productive way possible. Cliché as it sounds, it gets to the point where I can deliver that speech in my sleep. Well, not really, but you get the idea.

Apparently the same methodology worked for Tara Holland, who was crowned Miss America in 1997. Never surpassing first-runner-up status in various pageants beginning in 1994, Holland's determination drove her to acquire hundreds of local, regional, state, national, and global pageant videos, which she reportedly watched over and over. She studied each winner, watched them crowned, and envisioned herself in that position—over and over. When she finally won Miss America, three years after she appeared to be stuck in the "always a bridesmaid" pageant category, a reporter asked if she was nervous being in front of millions of people that night, ultimately achieving her coveted goal. Holland replied that she hadn't been nervous at all, and in fact winning wasn't a huge surprise. "You see," she said, "I had walked down that runway thousands of times before."[9]

The point is, preparation and practice enable you to achieve goals you once considered unattainable, or even unapproachable—such as being comfortable asking for a large premium. Though an inkling (or more) of discomfort may linger, as it did with me, in time, asking will not be a problem if you give yourself to the process. It became much easier for me as my business matured and I with it.

* * * *

9 Joel Osteen, *Your Best Life Now* (New York: Faith Words, 2004).

On the other hand, it's essential to understand that when asking for a high premium or anything else, you won't be successful with everyone. When that happens, and it will, taking it personally will only be damaging to your practice. It will set you up for failure.

The fact is, I consider myself an introvert with very thin skin. It bothers me when someone won't talk to me on the phone. Eventually it got to the point where I could force myself to make a cold call, but I still see that giant set of teeth about to clamp down on my ear.

It also bothers me when I make a presentation to someone after painstakingly analyzing their situation, proposing what I know to be the optimal pennies-on-the-dollar solution, and still they say no. I experience it as a personal rejection. After all those years in the industry, you'd think that feeling would have gone away, but we are humans, not machines. **With practice, I was able to train myself to accept a negative response, even using a no as a springboard to go back to the prospect three months or a year later and try again.**

Some of history's highest achievers are known introverts who had to overcome paralyzing shyness and sensitivity to accomplish what they did. Abraham Lincoln, Thomas Edison, Orville Wright, Rosa Parks, and even Johnny Carson were all admittedly shy individuals who were able to subordinate their fear of rejection to a greater cause.

Rather than taking rejection personally, if someone says no, as life insurance and financial service professionals we need to reevaluate that individual's needs and the proposal(s) presented to try to determine what was behind the rejection. Did we not make them understand the size of the problem, or that there was a problem at all? Perhaps they are in a position where they have no cash. Sometimes people have a tremendous net worth and millions of dollars in assets, but no liquidity. They have a multimillion-dollar problem that requires a very large premium, but insufficient cash flow to actually write the check. In fact, that individual has more of a problem than they realize.

If something were to happen to them, what will the company and their heirs do if a multimillion-dollar problem arises and they have no ability to pay for it?

If you don't take no personally, then you are able to take a step back and consider if there may be an issue that did not come to the surface, something the prospect did not feel comfortable divulging. Perhaps there's another solution, even inexpensive term life insurance, that can temporarily remedy the problem until the individual or company is in a better place financially. Term life insurance can buy time, and there have been many instances in my career where that's been a viable short-term solution. Some agents and advisors tend to scoff at the idea of writing a term life insurance policy, but I've always seen it as a prelude both to a more secure future for the client and to a relationship with me that can take them into proverbially greener pastures.

I make it my business to systematically follow up with a client for whom I write a term policy until I am certain the client is fully protected with a workable, permanent solution. On the path to making this happen, it is important that you check in with the client in an unobtrusive way, saying you are just interested in reviewing what's in place to make sure everything is working as it should. It helps make clear that you don't necessarily want to revise everything, but you do want to remind them that what you enacted was a temporary solution to a permanent problem. Chances are you'll eventually convert the term insurance to permanent life insurance. **But before you can do any of that, you have to make them a client, which opting for term life insurance can accomplish.**

One important example of my turning a no into a prelude to a yes involved a business succession planning client with eight family members in the decision-making process. Some were in favor of the solution; some were not. In this case, it was to be an $80,000 annual premium. We were also instituting a stock redemption agreement, so if the individuals died, the company would buy back their stock and family members would get the cash. The heirs would not have the burden of being involved in a business in which they wanted no part.

During this meeting, I felt like it was eight family decision makers against me. It was clear I had some convincing to do to overcome their objections. I told them to let me put things in perspective, asking what they were paying their senior line people on the floor. I also asked what they paid their custodians and other employees. When they provided the numbers, I immediately said, **"If you put me on the payroll for what you're paying your senior line manager, the day you walk out (my euphemism for the day someone dies) I'm going to walk in with millions of tax-free death benefit dollars to solve all the issues that need to be addressed."** I then asked if it really made a difference to the company's bottom line if they hired another "employee," to which they responded it didn't. That's what closed the case.

Another notable situation arose when I approached a prospect who was the CEO of a large HVAC company. Saying no came rather quickly on his part, but only because, as he explained, he'd already taken care of all the kinds of planning I was going to recommend. Seeing this as an opportunity rather than a closed door, I proposed that if he were confident all the right decisions had been made, maybe he wouldn't mind my reviewing the documents and providing a second opinion—gratis. He readily agreed, and when he produced the paperwork from a drawer, I observed that everything was marked "draft." Nothing had been signed!

As it turned out, his attorneys, with whom I later spoke with his permission, said they'd been urging him for two years to sign the documents, but with no success. After reviewing the documents, I observed that the laws governing the decisions made in the documents had changed, as had the needs of the prospect. In the end, because I didn't take it personally and stop at no, I acquired a new client.

· · · ·

Sometimes when agents and advisors work with prospects, they don't do the best job of putting the problem and solution in perspective. This in itself can garner a no, which is why it's worth examining.

If you've decided a million-dollar death benefit is warranted, and the prospect balks at paying the $40,000 which is 4 percent of the face amount of the policy, your reserve of examples can be called up, such as explaining that borrowing $1 million from the bank would cost a lot more than 4 percent—plus repaying the million. In this respect, the client needs to understand **they can either pay the bank or be the bank,** as that percentage is being built up in the cash value of the policy. In addition to a death benefit, it becomes a ready cash reserve for future use. It's incumbent upon the agent or advisor to communicate that while the problem may be complex, the solution is very simple. Once again: **the problem is the problem; the premium is the solution to the problem**. If the prospect doesn't accept the recommended solution, the problem not only persists but has the potential to destroy the individual, the company, and the family's financial security. Walking through a no involves finding ways to illustrate that the solution is what provides security, dignity, and peace of mind by putting a system permanently in place to address future issues.

There are times, however, when it is prudent to accept that, though you made your presentation, tried to explore, dissect, and address their objections, the prospect still isn't buying. It may be because it just isn't the right time or the right solution as far as they are concerned. Perhaps it wasn't even the right problem. Most of what we do is predicated on what the prospect or client is willing to share with us, and if their information is not fully disclosed, the solution will be off target.

There is also the factor of outside influences that prevent people from making decisions, or that steer them in a different direction no matter how airtight our solutions may be. There are times when no matter what you do, the outcome is out of your control.

We had an existing client for whom we were trying to do some additional work, but the client's in-house counsel ended up steering him toward another financial group. The other group was going to do exactly what we had proposed, and I couldn't figure out what had happened along the way. In time I learned that the in-house attorney had obtained some financial licenses of his own, and was in fact poised to receive a portion of the commissions from the other financial group. In a situation like this, despite the fact that it was an existing client of ours, we simply could not compete. Going back to the client, who we assumed was unaware of the fact that their attorney had cut himself into the deal, may have resulted in the total loss of that client. We didn't like it, but we had to accept it.

Most of the time, however, you approach a prospect with your entire arsenal. Every expert you know, every product you have, every ounce of preparation you've done, every planning solution you have, are all arrows in your problem-solving quiver. So you shoot your first arrow and you miss, but that doesn't mean you should stop. You pull out another arrow or two or three or six—whatever is comfortable for you, whatever it takes to earn the trust and confidence of the prospect or client. It doesn't always happen the first time, but as long as you can keep that door open, you can try again.

My business philosophy has always been that if they say no a third time, I'm going to find another prospect, but I may keep them on my mailing list. At the end of this chapter is a list of some of the techniques I have used to stay in touch with clients and prospects, some more innovative and attention-getting than others, but all of which maintain the connection. In terms of an all-out effort, after three earnest attempts I'm going to move on to more a receptive audience.

There are many agents and advisors who are like old bulldogs: they grab hold and never let go. That's perfectly fine if it works well for them, but it doesn't work for me. As a last-ditch effort when making phone calls, I may ask the prospect if I can stop in to introduce myself the next time I'm in their neighborhood, knowing full well I'm going to be in their neighborhood in a week or 10 days. But if they say no, that, as they say, is the end of that. Three is the magic number.

Just remember that whether asking for a large premium, persevering through a no, or determining what the right time is to let go, I cannot emphasize enough that preparation and practice are essential.

The following are examples of what I have done over the years to maintain contact and relationships with prospects and clients:

- Send articles and newsletters as an "FYI."

- Send birthday cards, either electronically or by snail mail.

- Send Thanksgiving cards.

- During the year-end holidays, do not send gifts to clients. Instead make a contribution to a charity in their name and send the client a letter to announce the gift. (I had a CEO client who once told me he received hundreds of business gifts each Christmas, which he tossed out or gave away. He owned everything and needed nothing, and barely even saw what came in. But when he got my letter that a contribution in his name had been made to a charity, he said it stood out and was the most significant gift he could have received. He would remember it, and me.)

- Mail Halloween cards. Hardly anyone does this. Include the client's staff.

- Most clients have gatekeepers, secretaries or assistants who have a great deal of control over who gets in to see the boss. If you use giveaways such as pens, keychains, and other items, make sure you give them to the client's staff. Next time you call, they will remember you.

- Handwritten notes on quality note-sized stationery will help set you apart from others.

- Use timely social media posts on a consistent basis.

CHAPTER 8

Don't Let Your Career Cost You Your Family

Remember, your children only grow up once.
You don't get a second chance to raise them.

In our senior year at Ohio State University, my soon-to-be wife Vicki and I sat in her apartment together, as we had throughout college, talking about our future. We'd known since high school we were going to be together forever, and we were designing what in retrospect I can see was a **life plan.** Alternating between healthy doses of The Beatles and Frank Sinatra on the stereo (the latter for ambience, naturally), the beautiful young woman I'd known since the second grade and I set about establishing our professional and personal goals. We defined the kinds of family values we both considered essential in raising what would in time be two dynamic, highly accomplished children. In fact, today they are both attorneys, which is why I can never win an argument with them.

No matter what you do in life, the legacy you leave is your family. Today, more and more Gen Xers and Millennials are choosing to plan their lives around a work-life balance that was not typically available to working parents in previous generations.

Building a career in the life insurance and financial services industry can be all-consuming—to the point where family becomes secondary or even an afterthought. The industry can take all your time and energy and exact a terrible toll if you let it. Because of its demands, I know agents and advisors who are on their second and third marriages (and in some cases, even those marriages are in jeopardy).

I know others in the industry who spent little time with their children while they were growing up. Don't let anybody tell you that "quality time" is more important than the quantity of time you spend with your family. It isn't. It's **the total time** you spend with them that counts. If you're going to teach your children about ethics, family value, hard work, the value of money, and the importance of doing a job well, you need to invest the time to do it—not just phone it in. You have to do it right the first time because you don't get a second chance to raise your children. The Million Dollar Round Table calls this the Whole Person concept, and I have been a strong advocate of this from the day I started my career, being a well-rounded individual who maintains a balance between family, business, and the community.

Let me share two stories about raising my children. One of the chores my daughters had to do was to occasionally help me wash the cars. They never enjoyed it because I made them follow certain rules, and they had to help me until the job was finished. After my daughters were grown and gone, one of them made a comment to my wife that washing the cars was never about the car. It was about doing a job all the way through and doing it right. It was a life lesson they didn't understand then, but do today.

During a spring break from college, our daughter Barbi was home with some friends. My wife was sitting around the table with them talking about life in general. All of Barbi's friends had come from broken homes and there was much talk of stepparents and stepsiblings. Later that evening, after everyone was in bed, Barbi came into our bedroom, crawled into bed with my wife, and said, "Thanks, Mom." And then she cried. The time and effort you invest in your family is well worth it.

Many years ago I was a featured speaker at the University of Oklahoma. Another individual spoke on the same platform, telling a story about how your children are like butterflies, flying high with lots of excitement. When you go home at night, and you've had a terrible, no good, rotten day, the last thing you want to do when your children come running to tell you about their marvelous day is push them away. You may be tempted to do it, but if you do, you crush them, just like butterflies, and that special moment of excitement for them goes away. Be careful you do not crush their spirit, excitement, and enthusiasm.

To help me remember this and keep my days in perspective, I put a butterfly sticker on my briefcase and on my cell phone. Every time I use my phone or pick up my briefcase, I am reminded of my children and grandchildren and how lucky I am to have a loving, caring family.

The way my wife and I handled the bad day issue was for me to call her just before I'd leave for home, telling her how my day had gone. If it had been a trying day for me, she'd tell the children their daddy needed a few minutes when he walked through the door to decompress. After going to our bedroom to take a few calming breaths, freshen up, and change clothes, I felt I could be a more attentive daddy for our girls, and I was ready to listen to their day. Those few minutes to myself and with my wife were exactly what I needed to transition to being fully present for the children. And, when necessary, our system worked both ways. I was always poised and ready to take the sting out of Vicki's day when she needed me.

As our children got older, my wife, who worked as a teacher when we were first married, then became my corporate pilot, and eventually got her financial licenses and went to work in my practice, and I decided that at all costs, we would be there when our children needed us, not just when we could work it in. Of course, being in the life insurance and financial services industry did allow us to make our own schedules. Even so, those schedules can get incredibly busy, so it's necessary to schedule family time and stick to it, barring occasional unforeseen circumstances. **My wife and children have always been my top priority**, and there were times when I was the only father at a school play or music recital because the other fathers worked nine-to-five jobs. I had some flexibility and chose to make what was important to my family a priority.

Our life plan included the opportunity for me to work long hours during the week, even into the evening, as long as I was home for Friday night dinners. Saturdays were spent with my wife (our "private time," or time set aside to socialize with other couples), and Sundays were family days, when our children got to choose what we all did together.

There are things I didn't do earlier in my career because I knew they would take too much time away from my family. These included serving on boards and committees, and even playing golf, which is irrefutably a time-consuming sport. When our children were older and more inclined to be involved in their own pursuits, I allowed myself more flexibility for outside activities, some of which served my business due to their networking potential, though I didn't participate in them for that reason. I did start playing golf at that point, but I have since stopped, which my golf partners thought was a good idea.

My father, who had quite a career in the life insurance industry, was from a different era, when parenting wasn't what it is today. He worked endless hours, 7 days a week, 365 days a year. Fortunately, my mother insisted he be at home for Friday night dinners and that we take family vacations, though these things weren't a priority for him. He was always absent from father-son banquets and other activities that would have filled the void I carry around to this day, so I made the decision that my children would always have my support and presence. My daughter Terri once gave me a plaque that said: "You're not only a role model for the industry, you're also a role model for me." As certain as I was before, from that day on I was even more confident that the way Vicki and I had raised our children was the right way.

* * * *

I tell people that in this industry to be successful you only have to work half a day. It doesn't matter if it's the first 12 hours or the second 12 hours. So when juggling work and family, time management skills are critical. There will be instances when you simply cannot avoid a weekend commitment, such as a meeting with a client who has moved out of state, needs to see you, and will only be in the area on the weekend, or some other unavoidable scenario, but if you have your priorities straight, those incidences should be few and far between. Most requests for meetings from clients can be channeled into days when you've not scheduled time with your spouse or children.

* * * *

Goal setting is quite important in this industry. You set one, then break it down into smaller components. In this manner, you learn what must be done every day, every week, every month to achieve it. Breaking the goal down into its individual pieces makes it much easier to accept and achieve. Sometimes achieving a goal means missing a family activity you may have set up, but if you've taken the time to educate your family about the industry and the way you work, you'll be supported in return. **You have made your loved ones members of your team, not just members of the family.** As a result, they've come to understand what it will mean to the family's future if they accept that you have to veer from the course on occasion.

Let's face it: work can be a war zone. Dealing with the public in our profession, all day long you hear the word no:

"No, I don't want to meet with you."

"No, I don't want this product."

"No, I don't like this suggestion."

"No, I don't agree with this solution."

The last thing anyone wants at the end of a grueling day is to come home to adversarial relationships and battles within the family—a kind of Midway in the hallway.

So often these situations are rooted in misunderstanding and lack of communication: "You never do this. You're never here to do that." Turning the domestic war of the worlds into less of a maelstrom and more of a mentoring situation, where your family understands that their help and understanding are what's important—and are given freely—can defuse the situation, or better yet, prevent it from happening in the first place. "What can we do to support you?" is immensely more pleasurable and productive than anything less.

Where my wife and I are concerned, we have always worked at maintaining open lines of communication with one another. If something was bothering one of us, we quickly discussed it to resolve the issue rather than letting it fester. I also believe that, during a disagreement, it's wise not to say the first thing that pops into your head. Once out, you can't take it back. Much like in a courtroom when something is said and a judge tells members of the jury to "disregard those remarks." There's not a chance that will happen. It's out there.

It really is important to think about what you are going to say before you say it, which is the road to no regrets.

In many circles, the thinking still persists that time invested in the family is time away from your business. Actually, that's not the case. When all's well on the home front, you are less distracted, more relaxed, recharged, and productivity levels rise. No one can be at the top of their game at one task or job all the time. I've said it before: we are not machines. **So in addition to maintaining close relationships with family, the variety and change of pace of spending time with them provides a balance**—and renewed energy and dedication when you are back at your desk.

◦ ◦ ◦ ◦

Real success requires excellence. There is little in this world that isn't about character, and part of that is striving for excellence. It informs the way we work and the way we live. It includes how we regard family. I hear people talking about "starter marriages," with the idea that it's not a permanent commitment. If it doesn't work with the least amount of effort, they're ready to move on to number two. That's not how my wife and I were raised, and we felt that neither family nor career should be conceived of in that manner. That way of doing things is devoid of character. It shows an absence of values, and it will make it difficult to be successful in life.

Everything you do should be about excellence. The work-life balance is important, and so is the depth and scope of your commitment to making it happen. When you operate that way in the world, you'd be surprised at how things fall into place. When all is said and done, the legacy you leave is your family.

CHAPTER 9

Never Put Your Needs Ahead of Your Client's Needs

Life is about helping others. If you are lucky,
you find a career that brings meaning to your life.

During a last-minute sweep of my e-mails before takeoff on a flight to Denver, I was momentarily distracted by the flight attendant's instructions. Though I'd heard these instructions many times in my 50-year career, this time they gave me pause.

Told to put on my oxygen mask first before helping a child or another individual with theirs, I was reminded that in the life insurance based financial services profession, the opposite is true. On an aircraft with a dwindling oxygen supply, it's clear you have to stay conscious to help anyone else. **But in our industry, putting your own needs ahead of the client's needs does a great disservice to them and may damage your reputation.** I've known too many members of this profession who were sued because they gave a client bad information when they allegedly knew better, or because of misconduct when they tried to cover up bad advice. And in the age of social media, someone you've not handled properly can destroy your career with a few well-strategized keystrokes in just a matter of seconds. It's out there, and it's intractable.

Let me begin this chapter by telling you that I'm a traditionalist. I like the old tried-and-true methods and would rather err on the side of being conservative. But I know that if I'm not out there looking for what's new, different, exciting, and cutting-edge, my practice will no longer be relevant and I won't be able to properly service my clients. On the other hand, my concerns have always been that while some of these cutting-edge ideas might work, the exposure for a client from both a tax and legal standpoint can be risky. And that must be measured against the agent's or advisor's own exposure for making a recommendation that may ultimately not work. This can be due to a change in IRS rules, state laws, or recommending a product or company that wasn't stable.

Throughout my father's long career, I saw steps that were taken for clients, whose needs we always put first, only to have the IRS come back and change things or for government regulations to change. Though what he (and my brother and I) did was appropriate at the time, they became difficult situations for us and our clients because we had to go back and try to find other products, and rewrite policies, at a time when the declining health of a client sometimes didn't provide the flexibility to do so. It wasn't because we had done something wrong or because the client had made a bad decision, but because rules and laws changed, and the assumptions made and formulas used were no longer valid. On top of all of that, had we made recommendations for solutions that didn't put the client's needs ahead of our own agenda, it would have added another layer of potentially serious problems in accountability.

The fact is, everything changes. Everything is fluid. **The key is being able to ethically defend your recommendations for solutions**

when they are held up to the light—or more specifically, the changing light—proving that what you did was in the client's best interest and not your own.

There have been many times when I've made a decision to leave money on the table knowing I could make substantially more commission if I steered the prospect or client into a different company or product. But had I done so, I would have obscured the options that might have been more appropriate for them. Say you are sitting across the desk from someone telling them this is what they need to do, and it's going to cost them $2,500 or $250,000 in premiums depending on the size of their problem. Perhaps for any of the reasons I've suggested in previous chapters, such as cash flow problems, they are not able to manage a premium of that size. But you continue to push hard anyway. You're not listening to what they're telling you. Perhaps you don't care enough to look for an alternative or interim solution because you are set on the higher commission when you close the deal. Maybe you convince them to pay it, but when the next payment comes due, they are so uncomfortable they don't pay it, and the policy lapses. So what have you really gained? You've lost 11/12ths of the commission *and* the client.

The questions then become "Have you been listening?" and "Are you professional enough to subordinate your needs to those of your client?"

Perhaps it's good to view term insurance as a "lease/option to buy" that can be put in place, because over time, it can eventually be converted to permanent life insurance. Remember: the first thing you have to do is turn the prospect into a client. But even if you do, should the premium be unmanageable, you'll end up with a fleeting relationship, as the client drowns in premiums they simply cannot handle. Earn their trust and confidence by taking smaller steps, no matter what you think it may cost you for now, and you can keep that door open for the future.

An outstanding example of the way this works is a policy I wrote for the son of a prominent client in the luxury goods industry. Initial coverage was written when he was a young professional with the goal of protecting his future insurability. The son didn't have the need for a lot of life insurance at that point, but his father, then the CEO, was savvy enough to know that as the second generation in the family business, his son would need much more down the road to run that business, collateralize lines of credit, support estate planning issues, and so on. The only caveat was that the son had to pay his own premium and had a nominal cash flow. We subsequently started the ball rolling with $1 million in term life insurance, which had a very low premium. The plan was that every few years, we'd go back in, review the son's cash flow, and convert 25 percent of the policy.

In time, the son acquired more responsibility within the family-controlled company and eventually became the CEO. Every year we converted 25 percent of the term until the full million was permanent life insurance. During the process we also added another $30 million worth of term insurance for this individual, as his value to the company clearly increased. That part of the term insurance is actually still in force. It is there to be converted as the client's economic picture allows, and this is a solid example of putting the client's needs ahead of ours. It is the magic of going the distance with term-to-permanent life insurance and how we get a client to the finish line.

This is also an example of how important it is to work with the next generation in a family business. Statistically, only 30 percent of businesses survive into the second generation, 12 percent into the third, and 3 percent into the fourth and beyond.[10] Many times this is due to a lack of planning and a lack of cash.

---

10 "Succession Planning," Family Business Institute, http://www.familybusinessinstitute. com/index.php/Succession-Planning/.

It's essential to invest the time in making the next generation feel comfortable with you, educating them along the way; making them understand what you're doing and why you're doing it. Naturally, all of this must have the parents' imprimatur, because on occasion they don't want the next generation to know some of the details, so you have to respect their wishes. But whenever possible, taking the steps to develop a strong business relationship with the next generation, and perhaps the one after that, is essential.

If you don't do it, then when the first generation dies and you've delivered the death claim, it's always possible that the descendant(s) will decide that since they haven't worked with you and don't know you, they will steer the business elsewhere. It may be to an agent or advisor from college, the golf course, or perhaps a recommendation from an attorney acquaintance of theirs. **Clearly, one of the keys to longevity in your business is to continuously develop and maintain relationships with the next generation in your clients' businesses who are on their own paths to success.**

❋ ❋ ❋ ❋

With few exceptions, it is mandatory to put the client's needs ahead of your own. But there is another story that should be told. This one about a time when it was not prudent to put the client's needs first. I include this because often new agents and advisors are so focused on accommodating the client, they don't consider all the possibilities.

Earlier in my career, I wrote life insurance policies for a heavy manufacturing steel-industry client. The senior family member was of an advanced age, and I was working with his son, the CEO, who was closer to my age. Having written a substantial amount of life insurance for the son, I had just made a presentation for the company to purchase life insurance for their CFO. At that point, my CEO client explained he was getting ready to take a trip, accompanied by the CFO. He instructed me to leave all the paperwork to be signed upon their return, whereupon it would be put in force. I recall thinking I should insist that everything be in place before they left, but I didn't want to push and impose on their busy schedules.

Unfortunately, both the CEO and CFO were on a U.S. Airways flight that crashed in Pittsburgh. Everyone on the plane was killed. I remember watching the news that day when an uneasy feeling went through me. I wondered if I knew anyone on that plane. Shortly after, the call came from the father that his son and the CFO had perished. I was one of the first calls the father made, knowing I'd been responsible for all of the life insurance planning for his son. It was a tragedy of immeasurable proportion for everybody, and it was also clear that because of the level of trust I'd cultivated with the family, I was one of their first calls.

We already had many millions of dollars' worth of life insurance on the son, so I delivered considerable insurance benefits to both the corporation and the son's family. But because I hadn't insisted on getting the forms signed and the policy in place before the client and CFO boarded the plane, I delivered nothing to the latter's family. I didn't do my job well enough to protect the CFO's family, something that haunts me to this day. It was clearly one of the biggest mistakes I've ever made, and my intention in sharing it is to prompt you to think things through at all times. Even something considered a real long shot like this can come to pass. And in the current age of terrorism, there is more at stake when it comes to travel. This increases the need to have everything in force as quickly as possible and to routinely update policies already in place.

For example, estate tax laws have changed a significant number of times over the years. They've increased, decreased, and even gone away. Earlier I talked about a client with a $34 million death benefit.

The client passed away in New York in 2010—a year when the federal government had eliminated estate taxes. So during that time there were no federal taxes to be paid, and the family retained all the money earmarked for this purpose. They still had to pay New York State taxes, but received an enormous death benefit to pay these taxes.

When we make recommendations to any client, we can only make them based on the laws at the time and what we can project based on what we're reading, studying, and hearing. That's also why it's so important to revisit clients every year or 18 months or so and tell them you need to review, not necessarily revise, what's in force to make sure it's still appropriate for their situation. Needs change. Businesses change. Families change. Laws change. Everything changes. Nothing is static, and you cannot rely on the client to call and alert you. Life insurance and financial services are not what they do, and they may not fully comprehend the issues, no matter how hard you work at educating them. Alerting you to any change is generally not first and foremost on their mind. It's your professional responsibility to monitor them.

Many times, I've met with people who'd had substantial policies written, and the agent or advisor never got back to them to do anything more. They simply solicited the business, wrote the policy, and walked away—sometimes years before. They received their commission and never provided a top level of service or any service for that matter. In these cases, the client doesn't have much loyalty if someone else comes in later. And even if you do provide exceptional service and follow up religiously, you'd better be transparent about and be prepared to defend the solutions you recommend. You don't want someone to come in behind you one day and discover something was not done in the client's best interest.

* * * *

Products, banks, broker-dealers, insurance companies, and others across the board are constantly in a state of flux—for better or for worse. Because of that, there have been times in the course of making recommendations to a client that I've been more concerned about the underlying financial stability of the entity I'm recommending than about the actual or projected performance of the products being used.

It's possible that, based on projections, a company has a product that looks quite good but their underlying financial ratings may be a little suspect. So the issue becomes one of the client outliving the company. If the company is not around at the time the policy turns into a claim, it does them absolutely no good. Sometimes even if the more stable, viable company's products are a little more expensive, or may not perform to the exact standards of some of the other products out there from the less stable companies, the client will feel more comfortable if you recommend the former with the explanation that it will likely still be there when it is needed.

Economics aside, there are times when putting the client's needs first can be very hard and presents a considerable challenge, but my philosophy is that it's incumbent upon the agent or advisor to ethically do everything in their power to fulfill the client's wishes, even if what they want doesn't come to pass no matter how hard you try.

In one particularly challenging incident, a longtime client in the trucking industry asked me to make some changes to a policy. The company I'd used to write the coverage didn't perform efficiently or properly in completing his requests, so the client blamed me because things just weren't getting done. I ultimately lost him because the changes weren't done in the manner in which he wanted and in the time frame he desired. You do the absolute best job you can, but the results are out of your control.

So, try as you might, putting the client's needs ahead of yours will not always yield positive results. But more times than not, it will, and it can create opportunities to expand their coverage and serve them for generations, and you will sleep well at night in the process.

I certainly have the same flaws as any human being. I am not immune to temptation. But I believe we are here to work at making ourselves better and help others in their pursuits as well. I've been very careful over the years to try to do the things that were right, as I didn't want to have to go home to my wife and children with apologies for something I fouled up, something that may have affected me and could have impacted my family even more. I didn't want to have to make apologies to my clients, my company, my community, or my house of worship for not exercising good judgement or acting in good conscience.

At times it was easy to subordinate my needs to those of my clients, but at other times it took real discipline, vision, and dedication. If you are a professional in this industry, putting your clients' needs first is the best way to succeed. Your actions are your legacy, and sleeping well at night cannot be overrated.

CHAPTER 10

Never Stop Learning—About the Industry and About Your Clients

One of the most recognizable attributes of professionals
is their willingness to continue to learn,
recognizing that they don't know it all.

We all knew him: the rudderless classmate in the back of the room who chose to do as little as possible, coasting through school in no particular direction, just getting through it. As the sayings go: You get out of something what you put into it. Nothing ventured, nothing gained.

Have you ever wondered where that individual is today? Short of the epiphany we can only hope he had, chances are he's not the CEO of a Fortune 500 company.

So what's the difference between someone who's just coasting through our industry and somebody gearing up to be a true professional? **The difference is the investment in learning.**

In the course of a year, we may need to call the customer service department of a cable provider or maybe a manufacturer about a piece of equipment or device we've purchased. The difference between a customer service representative that is fluent in their job and someone who is detached and stumbling through it is usually apparent in the first few minutes—maybe even sooner than that. Trainees notwithstanding (because we've all been there), it becomes abundantly clear in the course of conversation the level of somebody's product or services knowledge, along with their interest and willingness to spend time delving deeper into a problem in order to solve it. In short, there is a palpable difference between someone who has done and continues to do their homework and someone who hasn't. **It's the investment in learning that differentiates between the order taker and the true professional.**

In our industry, if you are not fully dedicated to your work, it's only a matter of time before your apathy becomes evident, as you will not be able to service your clients to the extent they deserve. If your focus is "What do I have to do to make a sale today in order to generate income?" and nothing more, you will not find the most efficient and effective solution for the client. An agent or advisor who embraces the industry in the interest of doing the best job for clients is always studying, always reading, learning, attending seminars, and going to their study group meetings because they want to develop into the best professional they can be.

They want to reach higher levels of professionalism and productivity. They want to make sure they master work-life values. They're always listening to everyone and everything because someone may say something that will trigger a particular thought or image that parallels a case they're working on, putting it into perspective, providing more for the client. Our industry is not linear. **Solutions come from all kinds of experience.**

So how do you keep learning? What forms does education take? I've broken it down into the following components, which may aid you in tackling it. Over time, you may come up with your own methods, but whatever works for you should become second nature—something you find a way to do every day of your career.

* * * *

IN THE BEGINNING...

If you're just getting into the industry, you may not have the rudimentary knowledge and skills you need. The first order of business will be to immerse yourself in whatever programs are relevant to the mentor or company with which you are working. It's important that you gain fundamental sales skills and basic product knowledge—just as great performers like B.B. King and Alicia Keys started with scales and world-class athlete LeBron James ran his drills (and probably still does). You can get to the top too, but just as they did, you must get the basics down first. I sometimes see new agents and advisors who immediately expect to achieve what their colleagues who've spent 10, 20, or 30 years honing their craft do, but that's unrealistic. You need to invest the time, and much of that time is spent learning.

Once you master the basics and you're out in the field calling on prospects and clients, it's time to ask yourself what can be done to increase your knowledge and skill level. You want to be better and better prepared to deal with the more complicated problems people need to solve.

I have several designations after my name: CLU, ChFC, RFC. These reflect years of study and testing, and even if prospects don't know what they mean, chances are their advisors—attorneys, CPAs, anyone in a position to endorse you—are quite familiar with them. While there are some designations that require only a few hours' worth of study and are subsequently frivolous, others demand a commitment of many months or years, along with comprehensive tests, before you can qualify.

If you're in the life insurance industry, the Chartered Life Underwriter (CLU) designation through the American College of Financial Services, also known as the American College, is widely recognized. It is similar to a CPA designation but for the insurance industry. The Chartered Financial Consultant (ChFC) designation, also through the American College, is something I highly recommend. Both the CLU and ChFC are the equivalent of master's-level courses. They are challenging to study and qualify for, and doing so proves that you're a dedicated professional in your industry.

Should financial planning be your goal, the Certified Financial Planner (CFP) designation is a significant credential. As does the American College, the College for Financial Planning offers the CFP certification; both schools are highly regarded in the industry. Multiple designations are recommended as you advance in your career. Just for the record, note that Registered Financial Consultant (RFC) is provided by the International Association of Registered Financial Consultants.

Again, these are all master's-level courses. There are PhD-equivalent courses as well as specialty courses for eldercare planning, annuities, long-term care planning, and many other areas of expertise. While you don't need them all, it's recommended to identify those that are going to best serve you and your clients and concentrate on them. There is a considerable investment of time and effort involved to obtain any of these designations; they can't be knocked out in a couple of months. Make the commitment and plan the time accordingly. **This, in itself, is part of the process of learning how to learn** so that you can keep on expanding the breadth and scope of your knowledge and your business.

• • • •

MANIFEST DESTINY: SEMINARS AND CONFERENCES

Seminars and conferences are a real gift to our profession, and there are many dozens offered each year. You may have to incur some costs when you attend those that are not available online, but the dividends can last years and multiply in ways you may not have imagined. In addition to learning directly from the experts about such issues as changing tax laws, new legislation, and anything else that may impact your career and affect your clients, the connections you make can extend your reach and increase the scope of your practice beyond expectation.

Rubbing shoulders with contemporaries in similar situations, or with specialties outside your realm, or agents and advisors in other regions of the country can start to expand your business exponentially. **While learning is the reason you're there, seminars and conferences are a kind of strategic manifest destiny in terms of cultivating external sources.** When a problem requires fresh ideas or a different direction, your sources are in place. Maybe it's something like the Johnny Appleseed school of thought—reaping from what you are so earnestly out there sowing.

While there are many more opportunities today than ever before to better your business in the form of TED Talks, podcasts, webinars, and other e-learning options, and I believe you should avail yourself of them as they suit your needs, that choice must be weighed against the advantages of actually attending industry events. Physical participation in seminars and conferences with their learning and contact opportunities may even help you make your way to the Million Dollar Round Table (MDRT), of which my father, my brother, and I were all members.

Founded in 1927, the MDRT is a global organization comprised of more than 42,000 leading insurance and financial industry professionals. It represents 470 companies in 71 countries. To become a member, you must achieve a certain level of productivity. Only the top 6 percent of industry professionals around the world qualify. There is also Court of the Table, where your commissions and income must be higher, about three times the basic requirements, and Top of the Table, where membership signifies you've made it to the top one-tenth of 1 percent of industry professionals in the world, at commissions and income six times the basic MDRT requirements.

Membership in the MDRT is a goal, and attendance cannot be replicated by anything offered online. When you get there, the elite in this industry are within reach, and bending their ears will take you further than anything else.

. . . .

THE GIVE BACK

On another level of learning, the first thing I did when I qualified for the MDRT was to volunteer my time for different positions within the organization. I made myself available to help run their meetings and annual conferences. The more you volunteer, the more you learn, and the more you learn, the more meaningful it becomes for you. I call it the "give back" as I don't believe in draining all the energy out of an organization without putting something back in. It serves you and others on innumerable levels.

. . . .

LEARNING OUTSIDE THE BOX

A 2012 article in *Psychology Today* talked about individuals becoming "observationally lazy."[11] While the term was used in relation to assessing danger and safety practices, I can extrapolate a bit and apply it to a learning technique I often employed to increase my business. The military calls it "situational awareness"; I call it personal observation. If you're looking to increase your business by learning more about what's around you, being lazy about observing what crosses your path can cost you.

If I was driving and observed an 18-wheel truck or a van with the name of a company on the side with which I wasn't familiar, and it had a local address, the first thing I did when returning to the office was begin investigating the details on the company. Who was the owner? Who were the decision makers? And was it a closely held company or one that was publicly held? (The former of which would have qualified it as a prospect.)

Before the Internet, we used Dun & Bradstreet reports and manufacturers' directories to ferret out this kind of information. I was looking for companies that typically did $5 million or more a year in sales, as they typically had $500,000 in bottom line profits or about a 10 percent margin. I was also looking for manufacturing-type companies, not retail organizations. In short, I was looking for businesses that were profitable, had sufficient cash flow to do what we needed them to do, and also had enough employees that there were one or two key individuals over and above the owners.

These were necessary ingredients to qualify for what my practice could provide, but it had to start somewhere. I would see a company

---

11 Joe Navarro, "Becoming a Great Observer," *Psychology Today*. January 2, 2012, https://www.psychologytoday.com/blog/spycatcher/201201/becoming-great-observer.

name on a drive back from a meeting or family event and use that as a green light to learn about the "suspect" who could later become a prospect and then a client. Everything was an opportunity to learn for me. It's important to never stop learning and never stop prospecting.

● ● ●

GALVANIZING GROUP

While I've mentioned it wasn't my style to use social occasions or other group activities to solicit business, I was a member of a highly focused study group for about 40 years. My study group, which is something I believe no viable agent or advisor should be without, was comprised of seven other like-minded individuals in the same age range, all New York Life agents. We worked in similar markets, though we were geographically diverse.

If I had a prospect or client in Ohio who had issues I did not know how to address, it was easy for me to pick up the phone and call my compatriot in Boston or in Seattle for direction and feedback. You study hard but you can't know everything. Because we met annually, our bond strengthening over time, my study group became my sounding board. You might say we were a band of business brothers (sisters would have been welcome, but in our case it was just brothers). **As I've said, you can learn from the mistakes of others, but you can also learn from the experiences of others.** Over four decades, each of us benefitted immeasurably from everyone else's work.

Though a study group can be organized in any way that suits its members, ours was highly structured in that we had strict bylaws and corporate charter, gathering annually in a different locale of that year's chairman's choosing. The chairman, who rotated among the members each year, was tasked with making all the arrangements: hotel reservations, dinner plans, outside speakers, the agenda. Our wives participated in separate spouses' sessions and the chairman's spouse set the agenda for them. The meetings took place Monday through Friday from 7:30 a.m. to noon, after which we were all free to go out and enjoy our surroundings, separately or together.

Topics over the course of the five days ran the gamut from becoming a better businessperson to improving levels of productivity; steps to becoming stronger professionals; how to deal with clients; how to run a business and manage our incomes and expenses; how to address problems we were facing that year; and where we found our individual success, to name a few. The rule was you had to attend this annual meeting with an open mind and a clean slate, allowing yourself to be transparent so that you could really benefit. I cannot recall a single year when I didn't come away with information that made me a better professional, business owner, husband, and father.

* * * *

FAMILY FARE

Part of being a true professional is the element of discipline. Parents use it when raising their children, but applying it to ourselves in the quest for learning sets an example our children can follow. While studying, learning, and really applying yourself can be measured in career results, the value of the seed it plants when children watch what you do is inestimable.

My wife, Vicki, has always said the reason our daughters have done so well is that they observed both of us improving ourselves throughout their childhoods. Vicki has gone from working as an elementary school teacher to a professional pilot to a financial professional over the course of our marriage, all of which involved a real commitment to learning. Now that we are moving toward our retirement years, she is substitute teaching to maintain learning and purpose in her life.

It wasn't just the nightly ritual of telling our children to do their homework while we went out to dinner or watched TV. It was the work ethic our daughters saw consistently, and firsthand, that serves them to this day.

 • • • •

At this point, if there is any doubt in your mind about the many advantages of continuing to learn, I recommend you think about the alternative. Not only is complacency a disservice to yourself, but everyone and everything in your wake loses out.

Yes, there are fundamentals you must master quickly to become a member of this industry, but this allows you to create exactly the life you want for yourself and your family by making a career-long commitment to learning and excellence. Just as the magic of life insurance creates something where nothing existed before, ongoing education creates its own kind of magic.

CHAPTER 11

Final Thoughts: Go the Distance and the Rewards Will Be Yours

"I can think of no more effective agent in advancing our freedom to live as we choose than the insurance salesman. This man knows the economic pulse of the country as few men may, for he walks all streets of American life and he sits down and talks to youth and to the mature and to the aged. He knows their wants. He helps them to help themselves in times of need. He builds, for he helps others to build. He insures the future. He is respected. And he is a friend."
—John F. Kennedy, 1963

Though President Kennedy made that observation more than half a century ago, nothing has changed. His words are even more cogent today when we consider the thousands of products and services available to clients through an evolving, all-encompassing industry. Life insurance, health insurance, disability insurance, stocks, variable products, indexed products, critical illness insurance, bonds, long-term care insurance, financial planning, managed money. Many of these financial options weren't available 30, 20, or even 10 years ago. What's on deck for the next 30 years may surprise us even more.

At the same time, the complexities of business, family life, technology, rules, regulations, and the law have increased. Today it is more incumbent than ever upon the agent or advisor to know how to make sense of everything in order to recommend optimal solutions to clients at all levels.

While a career in the life insurance and financial services industry allows us to live as well as we serve, in no way is it easy, and there are clearly no shortcuts. To truly help protect people and protect their businesses, assets, and families if they become disabled or long after they're gone, a consistent dedication to this profession cannot be overstated. If you are to become fluent enough to be able to insure the unexpected, a deep capacity to listen, a drive to learn, and an insatiable curiosity will produce remarkable—even magical—results. But the seed must be there and it needs to be cultivated. To be successful in this industry, you need to put that desire in the drinking water that's piped into your home. It has to be renewed every day and present at the cellular level.

Often, the problem with newer agents and advisors is that they have not experienced what it's like to deliver a disability benefit or death claim. Without knowing that feeling (and it is a deeply emotional experience), there may not be enough incentive to power through a highly competitive, challenging profession. They're selling life insurance and risk-based products for something that may happen down the road, but they may be 20 years away from paying that claim. Newer agents and advisors don't always get to experience sitting with a client, or a client's family, helping them through a traumatic event, assuring them that they are going to be all right financially because of the extent of planning that was done and the money that was created. The sense of fulfillment when things come full circle is indescribable.

When a client passes away, and you go to the funeral home, you see heirs and friends and other professionals: accountants, attorneys, and others. While they are paying their respects, they may also be wondering, "What's in it for me?" or more accurately, "What's going to be left over for me when the estate is settled?"

But you are not asking that question. There is nobody who walks into that room with cash in hand except you.

You're the one who has created the money that pays everyone else. You've made sure the estate is equalized and the family is secure and satisfied. You're the one who's guaranteed there's cash to pay the taxes so no one has to sell or liquidate at a loss. And every dollar you create will turn over in the economy six times. One hundred thousand dollars equals $600,000 to the local economy. One million dollars equals $6 million. Look at your book of business. Multiply that number by six. That is the impact you will have on your community over the course of your career. And when you see all that, when you see before you what you've done for the family and business and see it truly working, you know you did your job. You understand that all the years of studying and learning and implementing systems and investing and seminars and finding a work-life balance and building your business have paid off. **In one astounding moment, you know.**

For some agents and advisors, it may not take 20 years to experience this. There are unfortunate occasions when a client passes away or becomes disabled at a younger age, and that's also why we do what we do.

On the www.lifehappens.org web site, there are compelling examples of how life insurance and other products change lives in those instances, including the story of Jason and Nicole.

The young couple had a lot on their plate. As parents of a 2-year-old and with another on the way, Jason and Nicole—in their early 20s—were also juggling the demands of school, Jason's sales job, and running Nicole's in-home day care. Life insurance wasn't a topic they had thought much about, but when their insurance professional suggested a meeting, they sat down with him and listened.

The professional did a life insurance needs analysis, and while they did already have a little life insurance, it fell far short of what they needed. The couple understood how important it was for Jason, the primary breadwinner, to get more life insurance. But Nicole was adamant about getting a policy for herself as well. She wanted to make sure that Jason and the girls would be all right if something happened to her. While money was tight, Nicole said, "We're going to do this and make it work." So she incorporated it as just another item in their monthly budget.

Some years later, the couple stopped to help at the scene of a traffic accident. Jason, who had EMT training, ran to offer aid. Tragedy struck as Nicole tried to join Jason: A driver who hadn't seen the accident ahead changed lanes and hit her as she was crossing the highway. She was killed instantly. While life insurance will never bring Nicole back, Jason knows that without it they would have been in dire financial straits. The life insurance allowed him to take a significant amount of time off from work and be there for the girls as they moved through this tragedy. "People think, it will never happen to me," said Jason. "But my family is proof that it does. And you need to be prepared with life insurance."

There is another story of a young man, 27 years old, who appeared at a NAIFA (National Association of Insurance and Financial Advisors) conference and talked about his first job—and his agent. With full employee benefits, he had life insurance, medical coverage, some disability, and long-term care. Many people would consider this enough.

Walking across the street one day, the young man was hit by a drunk driver. His medical bills were in the $2 million range. Nobody is prepared to pay $2 million.

Prior to the accident, an agent had impressed upon him the merits of purchasing additional disability insurance, in tandem with what his employer provided, so that full coverage resulted. In the client's words, in the months following the accident he got to "retain his dignity" (and keep his truck, he proudly added!) in the face of unimaginable circumstances. This is what you can do for others as part of our industry. Provide security, dignity, and peace of mind.

· · · ·

Throughout this book, my mission has been to provide a blueprint of information, answers, real-life examples, ways to handle personal challenges, and effective work systems overall. These are the results of years of hard work and a range of experiences in this industry. My goal is to empower you with the tools to be as successful as you choose to be.

In **Chapter 1: Serve Well to Live Well,** I explained what the magic of this industry can do for clients—**creating money where none existed before**—and as a result, what it can do for agents and advisors who truly understand and work the profession. In times of tragedy or crisis, and for pennies on the dollar, clients, their businesses, and heirs can retain the security, dignity, and peace of mind they deserve because an agent or advisor has shown them how.

When you get better and better at what you do, because of the unlimited potential the life insurance based financial services profession provides, you can build a business of unimaginable proportions and create a lifestyle to go with it. As I mentioned earlier, according to the 2015 *Insurance Barometer Study* by Life Happens and LIMRA, based on 234 million adults age 18 and older, 43 percent (100 million) have no life insurance.

This is a problem—and an opportunity for you. The population base continues to grow. The middle class will move up the ladder. Fewer agents are serving them, so you have less competition and more prospects to work with. The opportunities to do well while doing good for others are unlimited in our industry.

In **Chapter 2: Six Systems for Success,** I showed you highly effective systems that have worked for me throughout my career. While you may develop some of your own, and I encourage you to do what works for you, I spent decades honing these systems. They address everything from severe call reluctance to extensive note methods, diligent follow-up, categorizing clients, delegating, and harnessing a team of outside experts that will help extend your reach. I also explained the significance of enrolling your family in your cause, making them as much a part of your team as anyone else.

In **Chapter 3: You Must Invest Money—and More—In Your Business to Make Money,** the concept of investing in yourself and your business was explained with points about state-of-the-art technology, conference and seminar attendance, the long-term benefits of hiring the right staff, and acquiring the right trappings, such as a well-maintained car and wardrobe.

If you are trying to persuade a client to purchase a product you do not have yourself, it probably won't happen. You must believe enough in what you are selling to own it. Just like anyone else, clients learn by example. If you invested in a whole life insurance policy that eventually provided a ready source of cash, say, to help purchase a home, provide funding for a spouse to start a business, or educate a child, there is no brochure you can hand to a prospect or client that can replace that kind of personal experience.

Chapter 4: You're Not Just Selling Insurance, You're Running a Business explored how to run an office, something generally not taught as part of agent or advisor training. Hiring staff that is a good fit for the way you practice, staff that works well together and to which you can delegate responsibility, is the key to building, sustaining, and growing a strong business. Just as important is the act of rewarding people for their work. For a variety of reasons, we replaced performance bonuses with salary raises, but you should do what feels appropriate for your business. If you want the best from people, make sure staff members know they are valued.

In running a business, **training clients is just as important as training staff**. Clients need to know from the beginning how you work. That per office protocol, their cases will be monitored by specific staff members who will stay on top of things. Their client load is smaller than yours, as head of the company (details about who is an A, B, or C client are your business, not the client's). Doing this right out of the starting gate will prevent a lot of misunderstandings and headaches along the way, which translates to time better spent on other pursuits.

Also in the realm of running a business is visionary budgeting. Due to fluctuations in client acquisition, the economy, and so much more, income can ebb and flow. Cash flow is typically not fluid. Whether your office is large or small, everything hinges on what you're doing, how you're doing it, what the commission levels are, when they come in, and so forth. Budgeting well is the answer, as well as having ready sources of cash in the form of bank accounts, CDs, lines of credit, and life insurance policies to use as collateral or from which you can borrow.

In **Chapter 5: The World Accepts Generalists, but It Embraces Team Leaders,** acquiring outside experts to augment your business was the order of business. While maintaining control is essential, losing the prospect or client because you tried and failed to do something that wasn't within your area of expertize isn't what you want. It's better to assess the situation going in, a skill you will develop as you become more seasoned in the industry, and defer to the experts you've brought on.

As a team leader, it's your job to find and cultivate these people for your team. Attending meetings, seminars, and conferences will help you do this. In addition to learning about new products, laws, regulations and the like, networking opportunities abound. If you have a study group, these are like-minded individuals you can trust and to whom you can turn for suggestions about outside experts as well. In some cases, I attended seminars for the sole purpose of learning something I believed I needed to know for my business, only to meet industry people during breaks and meals who actually offered much more to my business as experts later on.

In **Chapter 6: The Problem Is the Problem; the Premium Is the Solution—Not the Problem!** we saw that asking the right questions will almost always reveal the problem—even if the client is not aware they have it. If you are meeting at someone's home or office, photographs, plaques, trophies, citations, art, awards, and even a favorite old piece of sports equipment or memorabilia make for a great place to start the conversation and can reveal more about the prospect's needs and wants than a formal inquiry.

Devices such as an evolving **flow chart** provide great visual aids, displaying your products and services, as well as illustrating various scenarios where you might bring in an outside expert. Many people relate faster and better to something visual as it helps clarify what you are saying, which, try as you might, is often in a language they do not understand. At the very least, the flowchart reinforces your message.

Chapter 7: The Premium May Be a Bigger Deal for You Than for the Client identified getting out of your own way, if you are concerned about presenting the cost of a premium to a client, as the key to success. If the amount is something you are uneasy bringing up, a client may perceive that discomfort and it can affect the transaction, especially if you are addressing a problem they didn't even know they had. Discomfort can be construed as a lack of self-confidence, or a lack of confidence in the solution, and if you are not confident in your work, how can you expect results?

Sometimes agents and advisors look at the premium as the problem because they're concerned about how the client is going to be able to write the check. But as Chapter 6 spells out, **the premium is not the problem; it's the solution to the problem**. Without it, the problem doesn't go away and can, in fact, eventually destroy a company, its employees, and its heirs. The larger the company, the more accustomed its managers are to writing big checks, whether they are to retain key personnel, order inventory, or purchase life insurance or financial services products.

In appealing to a client, I strongly suggest rehearsing your presentation. Over the years people would listen to a speech of mine and assume I was a natural speaker—smooth and calm. But the fact is, I'd done my homework and had gone over and over and over the material until it was as natural to me as reciting the words to a favorite poem or lyrics to a song. The reason my delivery was close to flawless was because I'd studied, rehearsed, practiced. When you have what you think is a difficult number to present to a client, relentlessly practicing your delivery will transform the way you do it.

My father, hailed as one of the most successful life insurance salespeople in history, often rehearsed before a mirror as I sometimes do. While the technique is nothing new, it helped him reach the top, and it provides a level of confidence you can't acquire any other way.

If you had a role in a Broadway show, would you step out onto the stage for a performance without knowing your lines? Of course not, and your role in this industry is no different.

Do not underestimate the significance of **Chapter 8: Don't Let Your Career Cost You Your Family**. At the end of the day, your family is your legacy, and the gift of this industry is that it allows you to implement a work-life balance that may not be available in other professions. While there are innumerable cautionary tales of agents and advisors who did not agree with this, and lost their spouses and families in the process, enrolling your family in your cause, making them an integral part of your team, will yield exciting dividends for everyone.

Not only will you have the ongoing support and peace of mind you need to be truly successful without guilt or regret, but you will have a real partner in your spouse and, by example, raise your children to be caring, compassionate, conscientious, productive members of society. The MDRT calls this the Whole Person concept: balancing work, life, and success.

As **Chapter 9: Never Put Your Needs Ahead of Your Client's Needs** reveals, putting your clients' needs ahead of your own will help you build a powerful practice and peerless reputation.

Whether you are just starting out and money is tight, or further along in your career when expenses come up, there may be the temptation to go for the largest premium you can. It may be easy to rationalize that the client can afford it, but in the long run, decisions like this have a way of catching up with you. Any kind of conscious disservice to your client can impact or even destroy your career and the lives of those who care about you.

The life insurance and financial services industry is complicated. **It takes renewed dedication to studying and learning to stay abreast of changing laws, regulations, companies, products, and services in order to present the best possible solutions to clients.** This includes options like term life insurance, which, on the surface, may not appear to move your business ahead. But per the many examples I've provided, an immediate, less costly solution to a problem can turn a prospect into a client, even a lucrative client in the future, when term is converted to permanent insurance, and other products and services may be added as well.

Chapter 10: Never Stop Learning—About the Industry and About Your Clients is about making learning a priority. Learning will alter the course of your career toward success. I hope this book has been an invaluable learning tool and that you will add it to your education arsenal to use again and again as a resource. Let it be with you at every turn in the road.

For most people, there is no prototype for success. It is not a "one size fits all" proposition. In this industry, it is predicated as much on learning as it is on all the other things I've discussed. To choose not to make learning about the industry and about your clients a daily habit can be the death knell to your career. You cannot practice in a highly competitive, state-of-the-art environment when a lack of knowledge fails you and consequently fails your clients.

❊ ❊ ❊ ❊

If you're willing to go the distance, being a member of the life insurance and financial services industry is an unparalleled opportunity. In this profession, we solve problems for pennies on the dollar, creating wealth where none existed before, at a time when it's needed most. As an agent or advisor, you can create magic as long as you work hard, work smart, think big, and listen well.

* * * *

BEFORE YOU GO

A few years ago, I received a one-page description of life insurance titled "Just a Life Insurance Policy." The original author is unknown, but by the style and wording it appears to have been written decades ago. Regardless, the idea made me think of where our industry is today and where we need to focus our energy tomorrow. I've updated the description and offer it to you as a gift for choosing this industry—an industry you can be proud of.

I AM A LIFE INSURANCE POLICY

- I am a piece of paper, a drop of ink, and a few pennies of premium.

- I am a promise to pay.

- I help people see visions, dream dreams, and achieve economic immortality.

- I am education for the children.

- I am savings.

- I am property that increases in value from year to year.

- I lend money when you need it most, with no questions asked.

- I pay off mortgages so that families can remain together in their own homes.

- I assure people the daring to live and the moral right to die.

- I create money where none existed before.

- I am the great emancipator from want.

- I guarantee the continuity of business.

- I conserve the employer's investment.

- I am tangible evidence that a man is a good husband and father, and a woman a good wife and mother.

- I am a declaration of financial independence and economic freedom.

- I am the difference between an old man or woman and an elderly gentleman or lady.

- I provide cash if illness, injury, old age, or death cuts off the breadwinner's income.

- I am the only thing that you can buy on the installment plan that your family doesn't have to finish paying for.

- I am protected by laws that prevent creditors from assessing the money I give to your loved ones.

- I bring dignity, peace of mind, and security to your family.

- I supply investment capital that makes the wheels turn and the motors hum.

- I guarantee the financial ability to have happy holidays and the laughter of children—even though father or mother is not there.

- I am the guardian angel of the home.

- I am life insurance.

CPSIA information can be obtained
at www.ICGtesting.com
Printed in the USA
LVOW12s0947020617
536591LV00003B/19/P